The Elephant in The Bar

The Elephant in the Bar

How the Sexual Revolution Broke
Sex & Marriage
and
How to Keep It From Breaking You

Ron Jones

DEDICATION

To the couples who have shared their lives with me so freely and allowed me to see your true selves. It takes courage to open up our lives and examine what's really inside. All of you inspired me and all of you taught me. Each of you gave me more than I ever gave you. Thank you.

ACKNOWLEDGMENTS

Thank you to my wife Tina and my children, Nicole and Caleb. You are a joy and an education and an inspiration. I thank God for you. Living in a community of people is the only way to really live. I am blessed to have a real group of people in my life who fail and laugh and cry and rebuke and repent and celebrate and party with me. Some of you are in my local community and some live across wide distances, but you are with me and I am with you all the time. Each of you is reflected in all I've become and all I do. Finally I want to thank my friend Mike Wells who left us but never leaves us. He taught me to look for and expect Christ to be the center of all things.

CONTENTS

Introduction

I'm tired, so tired
I'm tired of having sex (So tired)
I'm spread so thin
I don't know who I am (who I am)

Monday night I'm makin' Jen
Tuesday night I'm makin' Lyn
Wednesday night I'm makin' Catherine
Oh, why can't I be makin' Love come true?

I'm beat, beet red
ashamed of what I said (What I said)
I'm sorry, here I go
I know I'm a sinner
but I can't say no (Say no)
Weezer – *Tired of Sex*

No one thinks these words will come true for them. Tired of sex?
How can that be? Everyone knows sex is the greatest thing on earth.
Every couple thinks they will never get tired of having sex. Couples
who've never had sex imagine how great it will be and how it will last
forever. Couples who are having sex imagine it will only get better.
Whoever wrote this song must have real problems. They sound like
they can't be committed to one person and they jump around having
sex with multiple people, so that must be their issue; that's why they
are tired of sex. But isn't it true that the way Weezer describes sex is
our culture's idea of sex? Have as much sex as you like with anyone
you like and don't let anyone try to tell you it's wrong. It is one of

our cultural "truths" that settling down with one partner, committing your whole life in marriage to one person, virtually guarantees you will get tired of sex. If we rewrote the song the way most people think about sex and marriage it would go like this:

I'm tired, so tired
I'm tired of waitin' for sex (So tired)
I'm spread so thin
I don't know who I am (who I am)

Monday night I'm beggin' Jen
Tuesday night I'm askin'
Wednesday night I'm askin' again
Oh, why did I ever marry that woman?

So which is it? Sex in any context makes us happy but keeps us from a committed relationship? Or a committed relationship will make us happy but kill our sex life? Our culture has lots to say to us about this; most of it confusing and some of it downright contradictory. One thing we rarely consider is whether or not we should be having sex at all, or if we are going to have sex, if there is an exclusive context in which to have it. The abstinence movement is mocked as foolish and unreasonable. Any suggestion there is a universal context for sex, which applies to all people, is ridiculous to modern Americans. But the failure rates of our most cherished relationships, our marriages, keep steady at 50%. Living together, delaying marriage, and testing our sexual compatibility early in relationships have been our primary answers to the divorce rate, but anyone who claims this is working is not honestly looking at the data social science has compiled over the past quarter century.

This is a book about sex. I know you probably know a lot about sex already. We are swimming in a culture soaked with sex, sexual information, and sexual imagery. You may think you are well informed about sex. You know about the mechanics of sex. You know how to avoid STD's and pregnancy. You may have a lot of first hand sexual experience. All of this is the window dressing of sex; none of it is substance. Do you know what sex means? Do you believe it has meaning at all? Or can it be meaningless?

I want you to question sex. Not just "should I or shouldn't I?" or "are my partner and I sexually compatible?" I want you to consider the role sex plays in your life; in your relationships. And it is playing a role even if you are not sexually active. The ideas you have formed and are forming about sex affect you. They affect your ability to have lasting committed relationships.

If you are in a relationship right now and have been for very long you know the pressure to have sex, not have sex, or keep having sex. You feel it as more than just physical attraction, you feel it as social pressure. If you are not in a relationship you know sexual expectations go along with entering relationships and you have to navigate those expectations to get into one. If you've been sexually active with several partners over several years you are faced with conflicting feelings about the meaning of sex in past relationships versus it's meaning in current or future relationships.

In this book I'm going to help you question the attitudes you have about sex, including the attitude that monogamous, non-marital, or pre-marital relationships are healthy environments for sex. I'm going to suggest the exact opposite of the cultural message that marriage ruins your sex life; I'm going to tell you that sex is ruining your married life. By that I mean your beliefs about sex, not just your actions, are ruining your chances of finding what all of us want: a life-long, committed, loving, marriage.

I don't expect you to be happy with me for making the suggestion. I understand. We have strong opinions about sex. But what if we are wrong? What if sex is deceiving us? What if it's like this:

A man goes into a bar in Ireland and orders a Guinness. The bartender reaches under the counter and takes out a little brown paper packet full of powder, tears it open, pours it out on the bar, and then serves him a pint.

The man says, "What's the powder for?"

The bartender says "This is a very good powder, very expensive. If I spread this powder on the bar before I serve a Guinness no elephants will ever run through the bar."

The mans says, "But there are no elephants in Ireland!"

The bartender says, "I know. I told you, it's a very good powder!"

The bartender is deceived. He is spending money on a powder with no power, and someone is making money off his deception. He never questions the effectiveness of his powder. It works. Everyone can see it works. No elephants ever come into the bar! The only way to help this bartender and undeceive him is to bring an elephant into his bar. It is the only way to get him to look at the powder with fresh eyes.

There are problems with elephants coming into bars. They break things and push things out of place. They disrupt business as usual. We understand why the bartender doesn't want a big smelly beast in his bar. He probably won't appreciate it if you try to bring in an elephant. He may fight you.

Is it worth the trouble to attempt to undeceive him? It depends on how much the powder costs. If it's cheap powder it may not be worth it. But what if the powder is costing more than the bar makes? What if he pays so much for the powder he can't afford to eat or pay his bills? What if buying the powder is bankrupting the bar? Getting an elephant into the bar is worth all the expense and disruption. Getting an elephant into the bar is saving the bartender's life.

We live in a culture where more and more people believe in the power and importance of sex without questioning it. We also live in a culture where broken relationships are an epidemic. You want to go the distance with your relationship? You have to seriously question the role of sex. You have to look at the promises sex makes to us and if it keeps them. Your ideas about sex – your firmly held beliefs about sex – may be setting you up for failure. You may have to have an elephant run through your bar.

Reading this book may push some of your mental furniture out of place. It may stop you from business as usual in the bedroom, and it might be messy. It may also save your life. I hear you saying: "Save my life?" Yes. Not in the "pull you from in front of a speeding train" kind of saving, but in the sense that your beliefs about sex – your deceived thoughts about sex – are killing your real self. It could be that your beliefs about sex are bleeding away your life; your real joy, your real identity, so that slowly you find you've expended your self; years are gone and can't be recovered; and your most important relationships are permanently damaged.

The trouble with being deceived is that you are deceived. We are all blind where we are blind. Sex has all the characteristics of something that can blind us. It affects not only our bodies, but also our minds and our emotions. It can immerse us and isolate us from reality. Have you ever had really mind-blowing sex? Something you felt was the best sex of your life? A mountaintop experience? What if it was really only a molehill? On the other hand, have you ever had a really bad sexual experience? Have bad sexual experiences piled up on you and convinced you that sex itself is bad or that you are bad at sex? Are you afraid of sex or afraid you won't be good at it? Do you feel like you are the only one who isn't having sex and you are missing out?

What if you are missing out on the real point of sex altogether? What if your expectations and your experiences are both deceptive? It would be better to know the truth about sex wouldn't it? It would be better to know your great sex is only vanilla ice cream and Rocky Roads is a possibility. It would be better to get rid of sexual guilt or shame, and it would be better to stop expecting sex to give us things it cannot give. It would be freedom; freedom to experience great sex, and great relationships.

If you are deceived I'm not judging you. I've been deceived about sex, and it caused me a great deal of pain. I've spent hundreds of hours counseling couples about their relationships and found every one of them suffering from deception in one form or another regarding sex. There's no shame in finding out you've been deceived by sex; but don't stay deceived.

If you are skeptical about the claim that sex might be deceiving you and damaging your chances at having the long term, loving, committed relationship you want, you may ask, "Is there any proof (i.e. empirical evidence)?" Great question. Lets begin here and see what we find.

Chapter One

Ten Myths We Believe About Sex and Relationships

*I don't wanna know
what I know to be true
What I need you to do,
tell me another lie*
- NE-YO, *Lie to Me*

*Do not deceive yourselves. If any of you think you are wise by the standards
of this age, you should become "fools" so that you may become wise.*
Saint Paul, 1st Letter to the Corinthians 3:18

Flipping through channels last weekend in the midst of a sports
drought, I found *The Shawshank Redemption.* The odds are that if you
channel surf next weekend you'll find it too. *Shawshank* accounted
for 151 hours of airtime on basic cable last year. That means it ran at
least once a week every week on some cable network. People can't
get enough of the story of the wrongfully accused Andy Dufresne. I
love the story too. It pulls me in every time I see it. I want to linger
in it. Even though I've seen it a hundred times, there are some
scenes I just have to watch. Like the moment Andy crawls out a
sewer pipe into the pouring rain, and holds his hands up to the sky, a
free man.

Stories are powerful. Sometimes we choose to live vicariously
through stories, imagining ourselves within them. We also *live out*
stories whether we know it or not. We find roles for ourselves. We

find scripts that go with our roles. Families shape stories for most of us. If you were the first child born to your parents it's likely you are more driven and goal oriented than subsequent children. If you were the baby of the family, there was a different set of rules for you. Both roles come with scripts.

We can reject the scripts our family hands us, but it takes effort. It takes a revelation too; a revelation that we *are* playing a role. It's not something we can see on our own because, unlike a casting call for a role in the class play, these roles and scripts are invisible and we've had them from birth. Some roles the family gives us are positive, like being the "hero" or the "achiever." Some are not so good, like being the "goat" or the "under-achiever." Reaching escape velocity from a family script is challenging because of the pressure we get from family members. When one of us challenges the family story line it means all the other players have to reexamine their own roles, and that is uncomfortable.

There are other roles we play and scripts we read outside our families. There are cultural roles and scripts. Cultural roles may be harder to escape than family supplied roles for two reasons. First, these roles are so widespread, and so many of our peers play them, that practically no one recognizes them as roles. They are "just the way things are done." Second, the sheer number of people using the scripts and playing these roles weighs heavily against anyone who tries to depart from them. As a result, most of us live our roles and read our scripts without much reflection. Many of us do this even though we don't like the roles and know we don't like them – we just can't see any other way *to be*.

We may go to college even though we hate school, like working with our hands, and would be happier going to a technical school. We may delay getting married even when we are sure we've met the person we want to marry. We may have sex with people even though we aren't interested in being intimate with them.

Cultural scripts and roles, like our family scripts and roles, aren't necessarily bad, but they can lead us to make decisions based upon ideas that are demonstrably false. This is never so true as the roles we play and the scripts we read from with regards to relationships and sex.

In their 2011 landmark book, *Premarital Sex in America: How Young Americans Meet, Mate, and Think about Marrying*, authors Jeremy Uecker, a sociologist and assistant professor at Baylor University, and Mark Regnerus, a sociologist and assistant professor at the University of Texas, list ten current myths about sex and relationships. The authors say this about these myths:

> We call them myths because the empirical data from surveys and interviews suggests they aren't true most of the time. In other words, these ten myths may be believed by many emerging adult men and women, but the evidence supporting them just isn't there.

What do you call something you believe without empirical evidence? It depends. Our culture is thoroughly secularized – we demand empirical proof to back up claims about truth. Religious people are criticized and/or marginalized because they offer no empirical proof for their beliefs. People of faith are thought of as less intelligent, gullible, or deceived because of this. Belief without evidence is foolish in our culture. Yet the following ten ideas are believed by the majority of young Americans with no empirical data to back up their beliefs. Here are the ten myths compared to what the data shows.

Myth #1: Long-term exclusivity is not possible or desirable.

Data: Long-term exclusivity (marriage) is possible and also what the majority of us seek.

Myth #2: You have to introduce sex to sustain a new relationship or help a struggling relationship.

Data: Waiting to have sex is the best thing to do if you want a long term, stable relationship. The longer you wait to have sex the better your odds of sustaining your relationship. Introducing sex does not help struggling relationships.

Myth #3: The sexual double standard (men and women experience sex uniquely) is inherently wrong and must be resisted by any means.

Data: The sexual double standard is inherently human because men and women are unique in their sexuality and experience sex accordingly. Trying to make women treat sex the way men treat sex or make men treat sex the way women treat sex does not work – it's like trying to get a dolphin and a horse to experience water in the same way.

Myth #4: Men can't be expected to abide by the sexual rules women may wish to set.

Data: Men will abide by the sexual rules women set. Women are the sexual gatekeepers and can determine their own terms for when sex should start in a relationship. Men will wait or not wait for sex depending upon what women decide to do.

Myth #5: It doesn't matter what other people do sexually; you make your own decisions.

Data: It matters very much what other people do sexually. When many women flood the sexual marketplace with relatively low cost, low commitment sex, and when many men access cheap pornographic sex, everyone is affected. Based upon what people are doing sexually today, new norms are established and the market adjusts to the new conditions.

Myth #6: Porn doesn't affect your relationships.

Data: Porn affects your relationships, and affects all our relationships through changing perception and expectations for sexual activity.

Myth #7: Everyone else is having more sex than you are.

Data: Everyone else is not having more sex than you are having, even though everyone believes everyone else is having more sex than they are having.

Myth #8: Sex doesn't have to mean anything.

Data: Sex means something, always, every time, without exception, even if a single sexual act appears to have no meaning, because the accumulation of sexual acts affects us.

Myth #9: Marriage can always wait and should wait until we are stable and/or successful.

Data: Marriage can't wait forever. There is a market of marriageable people and it decreases over time leaving less and less desirable candidates available, while we ourselves become less attractive candidates.

Myth #10: Moving in together is definitely a step toward marriage.

Data: Moving in together is not necessarily a step toward marriage and is more likely to lead to break up than to marriage.

Note: for a more extensive discussion of data and Social

Sciences see Appendix B and for more on the 10 Myths see Appendix C

People take these myths on faith. They are part of the story our culture gives us; the story many of us live; the script we read. And they are wrong. They don't stack up against the evidence.

We are rational people, right? We should be able to take stock of the evidence and act in ways that make sense. But we don't. Large numbers of us live with these myths not only as *true*, but as *unassailable truths* – things that are not to be questioned; beliefs so strongly held that any evidence offered to the contrary is dismissed out of hand. This is what we expect out of religious beliefs, not beliefs about sex and relationships. This is sex elevated to a religion. This is sexual dogma; and most of this dogma is relatively new. It is true that sex as a deity goes back to the dawn of man and is found in many cultures, but American attitudes toward sex and relationships have changed rapidly over the past 50 years. These embedded beliefs we take for granted were not the beliefs of our grandparents. What happened?

We need to look at who benefits from these beliefs, why they would promote them, and why they would want to keep them alive. By all measures the people who benefit most from the perpetuation of these myths are men. Traditionally, women were in control of sex. Women decided when sex began in a relationship. Women decided what they demanded in exchange for sex. But that began to change in America in the 1970's.

The sexual revolution of the 1970's is a primary source for the 10 myths. Many believe the sexual revolution was a movement by women, for women, that it liberated women sexually and gave them more choice in matters related to sex and relationships. As Regnerus and Uecker write in *Premarital Sex in America*:

> While women have fought a long and noble fight to
> enjoy greater equality with men, we're not sure that

the struggle has paid off in the domain of sex as it has in education or the workplace. Women are now freer to have sex like men, but most—if they're honest with themselves—don't wish to.

When we examine simple connections between recent and lifetime sexual partnering, frequency of sex, and a variety of emotional-health indicators— including depression scales, self-reported episodic crying, life satisfaction, depression diagnoses, and current use of prescription antidepressants—it quickly becomes apparent that having more numerous sexual partners is associated with poorer emotional states in women, **but not men.** (emphasis added)

Fifty years into the sexual revolution, the throwing off of "traditional" views of sex along with how we view gender roles, is working out great; if you are a man. Men who used to pay a much higher price in terms of commitment and stability in order to gain access to sex, can now have sex for little or no commitment. Women, who were encouraged to view their sexual decisions in a "liberated" way (i.e. to have sex when they wanted with whoever they wanted) are not faring so well by putting that into practice.

In the traditional view of sex, women were the gatekeepers who could demand relational security in exchange for sex, and men were the pursuers, exploring the "market" for the "price" they had to pay for sex, and trying to have as much of it as they could get for the lowest cost. As more women adopted liberal attitudes toward sex, the market slowly started to flood with lower cost sex in terms of commitment.

Today a woman who withholds sex from a man is no longer an obstacle for him – he has plenty of options readily available. Men can have sex for next to nothing with many partners – literally a school boy's dream, and they are doing it with abandon, and, evidently without causing themselves much long term damage. Women on the other hand, are not faring so well.

It makes you wonder whose idea the sexual revolution was in the first place, and what they hoped to accomplish. It was all couched in such inclusive terms when it began – why shouldn't we all stop feeling guilty about sex and relax? Why shouldn't women be able to have as much sex as men are having? The truth was (and still is) that men were not having more sex than women; that single men always had (and still have) less and less satisfying sex than their married friends, and that women enjoyed sex more when they had greater power over the sexual market place by rejecting casual sex and waiting for sex in an emotionally stable relationship.

So we can account for the emergence of the ten myths to a great extent, as the result of the sexual revolution. On it's own, though, it is doubtful the sexual revolution could have produced and maintained the myths, but the sexual revolution gave birth to a problem child that changed everything. It created an environment ripe for the acceptability and mainstreaming of pornography, and coming of age at the dawn of the Internet, porn has grown into the third wheel in the bedroom in all of our relationships. Porn is everywhere. It is the one factor driving the "price" of sex down, and utterly changing the sexual marketplace.

Studies show that men are physically satiated through the use of pornography to a level that rivals sex with an actual person. In terms of commitment to a real person, which was the traditional cost of sexual satisfaction, men can now receive sexual satisfaction for zero commitment to a real person. Again quoting Regnerus and Uecker:

> Since high-speed digital porn gives men additional attractive sexual options—more supply for his demand—it by definition takes some measure of price control away from women. As a result, the

cost of real sex can only go down, taking men's interest in making steep relationship commitments with it.

Porn shapes expectations, even for men and women who never use it personally. We are surrounded by people (the vast majority being men) who do use it regularly. Men who use pornography accept what it gives them as reality. They feel the sensations of sex without the experience of another person. They believe it is real. They think real women can and should do the same things they see in pornographic videos. If women don't perform sexually the same way porn women do, digital reality is only a click away. This cyber-sexuality leads to men who are less and less motivated to work on relationships that do not include readily available, fantasy-like sex. Of course this is all a great hoax and pornographers are happy to keep up a steady supply of plastic sexuality to paying customers.

Women notice the effects of the widespread use of porn in many ways. They realize men are less interested in them and less motivated to give them commitment. They see that men do not notice them when they wear normal clothing and that men do notice women who wear clothing that once would have been considered too provocative to wear in public. Those who enter sexual relationships find they are expected to perform like porn stars. Women respond to all of this by lowering their demands in order to get what they want. Men who would otherwise not be attractive candidates for a relationship are now hot commodities if they show up on time for a second date and wear clean clothes. Porn has literally flipped the script.

So where does this leave us? Men and women now relate to each other and have sex with each other based upon a new script. Modern women, the daughters of the sexual revolution, are supposed to be free to act like men – to sleep around – but this harms them. Modern men, programmed by pornography, are Novocained toward relationships and misguided about sex with real women. The data is clear; sexual liberation was supposed to get us all out of prison, but unlike Andy Dufresne, we crawled through a sewage pipe and fell into a sewer, not a cleansing shower of fresh rain.

The answer to our first question is yes, there is good empirical data to suggest we are deceived by sex. The data shows these myths are hurting us. If we are deceived about sex and relationships it implies there is something we are missing. I'm going to take you on what may seem like a detour. I realize that even when presented with the facts, most of us feel we are the exception. We think our relationship is different from all the others, and we know what we're doing. You are right. You're a unique person and your relationships are unique. Go back to the beginning question. What role does sex play in your relationships? If it is a deceptive role; if it is telling you your relationship is perfectly solid when it's not, you need to find out so you can have what you actually want: a lifetime with your partner. So don't stop here, take a look at the real depth of sex, the real meaning. It will be time well spent. I promise.

The stunning truth you must face is this: either sex is much deeper than you ever imagined, or it is as shallow and meaningless as a pornographic video.

Next question: Is sex about biology or something more?

Chapter Two

SEX IN THE WILD KINGDOM

You and me baby ain't nothin' but mammals so
Lets do it like they do on the discovery channel
-The Bloodhound Gang, *The Bad Touch*

You are not your own; you were bought with a price.
Therefore honor God with your body.
Saint Paul, 1st Letter to the Corinthians 6:19-20

A few years ago, driving a school bus for the city, I entered a parking lot where 15-20 buses regularly park. It was 430 in the afternoon. I had just finished the afternoon run. I passed a line of parked cars on the way to my parking spot, and out of the corner of my eye I saw a couple in a compact car. It was just a glance, but in my head I thought, "Oh my gosh, they are having sex right there, right now in that car!" I parked my bus and thought about it. It seemed so odd. Was I seeing things? Would someone really choose to have sex in this place at this time? It was so stupid it was almost unbelievable.

Getting in my car I was conflicted. I'm a "mind my own business" kind of guy, but this was so weird. On top of that, what was I going to do if they were having sex? Go up and knock on the car window and break it up? I drove slowly behind the row of cars till I was directly behind the car. It had a vanity plate, I noted, and yes, a couple was most definitely "making each other happy" in the passenger side seat. Just as I pulled up the girl, who was perhaps 15 or 16 years old, looked up. For a second our eyes met. She was surprised, and embarrassed and so was I. She buried her head out of view. I hesitated, wondering if I should do anything, and then drove away.

What should I have done? Did I do the right thing? I told my wife about it that night. She said something about how brazen kids are these days. The incident stayed on my mind. It kept coming up and I kept trying to forget it. That young girls face haunted me. It wasn't just embarrassment in that face. It wasn't getting caught. It was the lack of joy. It was embarrassment overlaid upon emptiness. My heart hurt over that look.

What difference does it make? I asked myself. These aren't my kids and I'm not responsible for them. They wouldn't listen to me even if I tried to talk to them. The feeling wouldn't go away, though, and so I found myself at the end of the week cruising through a local high school parking lot looking for a little white Honda with a vanity plate. I figured it must be high school kids – who else would be that dumb or that broke to use a public parking lot for their sexual exploits?

The first high school I visited turned up nothing. I thought I might be able to forget about the whole thing, but a few days later I felt compelled to try the other local high school. There, second row back from school in the student parking lot, I found the Honda with the matching tags. I felt like a stalker. And I thought what a really awkward story it would be if a middle-aged bus driver was discovered tracking down some high school students because he'd seen them doing the nasty in a bus parking lot. Can you say "fired" and "law suit" in one quick sentence? I thought, OK, now what am I supposed to do? I went over the facts again. I witnessed two people having consensual sex in a public parking lot. They turned out to be minors. I have no connection to these people other than them deciding to have sex where I park my bus. That's it.

If we're just mammals who happen to be the most evolved creatures in an accidental universe, why does it make us feel weird to see a couple of our young copulating in a Honda? It's just a fancier, mobile cage, and they are no different than monkeys. So what? Would this situation make you feel awkward too? Or would you pull up beside them, eat some peanuts and watch?

Two things stand out to me about this scenario; first, I don't believe many people would actually engage in sex openly and publicly, and second I'm sure people would not stand by idly and watch other human beings having sex publicly. But why? Surely it's more than clothes covering up our reproductive organs that separate us from other creatures. I've never been to a nudist colony, but I imagine public sex is frowned upon in that environment also. Yet there is no such reticence on the part of any other creature. Have you ever heard of dogs that only do it in the doghouse? Or raccoons that only do it at night and out of sight of their young? No. We wear clothes and we keep our reproductive organs and acts to ourselves.

We are going to look into the claims sex makes; what it is selling us. First we have to decide if we are really just mammals with hang-ups or something else altogether. This is the point where we decide if there are any elephants to let in the bar at all.

How did we get so neurotic about sex? If we believe we're the most highly evolved creatures in a world guided only by natural selection and survival of the fittest, we have to account for our sexual attitudes one way, but if we are something else; if we are creatures of a creator who not only placed a genetic code in us, but also placed a code of behavior in us, we have to account for our sexual attitudes in a completely different manner.

Looking at ourselves as strictly biological entities leads to some immediate problems. The facts are that people do not act sexually like any other creatures that we know. No other creatures wear clothes. None hide their sexual activity. Few species are exclusively mated for life, or show any signs of distress over partners who switch from one sexual partner to another. We have no indication that any other species has sex exclusively for pleasure. Animals don't use birth control to keep sex from producing offspring. No other species produces pornography. Animals don't spend time in therapy because they've become sexually dysfunctional. No other species produces drugs that will allow sexual activity to continue well beyond their normal reproductive age.

Those are some significant differences to account for in the evolutionary scheme of things. If you embrace naturalism as your truth; that humans are simply the best biology on the planet, survivable, and durable, you have to account for these differences as things that provide evolutionary advantages. Once you do that you must use it to account for the way you feel when you see people having sex in a car in a parking lot, or when your sexual partner has sex with other people, or when you can't perform sexually. If we are just biology, our feelings about sex are also biology and couldn't be different than they are. They exist because they exist. That's it.

If we are just biology, none of us has any authority to tell anyone else how to behave sexually. Each biological unit performs according to its nature which is part of NATURE and we don't really know how NATURE is using a particular action to render the best outcome for a species. In fact, why should we believe NATURE favors humans at all? There is no guarantee at all that humans will remain at the top of the food chain. Maybe another species is evolving to replace us and so our attitudes and actions are part of tearing us down in preparation for a new dominating species for the planet. In short, if biology accounts for everything, it can account for EVERYTHING. That means it can even account for our accounting. Our neurotic sexual activity isn't neurotic because there is no such thing as neurotic; there is only biology doing what biology does. A human being is no different than a dandelion and grows exactly the way it grows for the same reason the dandelion does. We may not like what dandelions do to our yard, but no one seriously attempts to tell a dandelion to stop spreading its seeds in the wind.

If we are looking for answers to our sexual problems or just for help in understanding sexuality, biology and evolution gives us answers, but they aren't much help it seems. Biology says you feel the way you feel because you feel the way you feel and it couldn't have been any different. Evolution says sex is part of nature and so is our understanding of sex; no attitude toward sex is right or wrong and no conclusions we draw about sex can be right or wrong either. It's all part of evolving.

So there's no elephant here, is there? Nothing can upset you or push things out of shape for you if you embrace yourself as merely biological. Do what you want and believe what you want because it really doesn't matter. This is the Blood Hound Gang view of sex: Nothin' but mammals.

What about the creature/Creator view? It is worth noting that, in general, people who truly embrace the evolutionary point of view, place the blame for sexual problems in the lap of those who embrace this second view. Religion, they say, is the problem that creates sexual problems and gives us hang-ups. They fail to recognize that, if they are to remain consistent, religion is also part of evolution and biology. If biology is all we have, religion is evolution too! It can't produce problems because there are no problems. Maybe it will go away as something that was temporarily useful to our development, but complaining about it is just talking to dandelions.

But what if there is a Creator? If there is a Creator who imprinted us with characteristics unique to humanity we can begin to explain our sexual behavior and attitudes much differently. We can use these things as clues to discover what kind of Creator we have. Why is our sexuality different from other creatures? What are the implications of having a God involved with our sexuality?

The first thing we need to grasp is this:

If Creator, then purpose.

When you see a hammer for the first time you may admire it for a while, but eventually you ask, "what is this for?" "What was this designed to do?" Try to imagine a created thing that has no purpose. Look around you. Every thing you see was created with a purpose. From pleasure to information to work, all "made" things are things made with purpose.

Having a Creator means sex has a purpose, and that purpose originates with the Creator. Sex was thought up, designed and implemented for a reason. It isn't an accident, it is a design. Why is that so important? If sex has a purpose, it can be used correctly or incorrectly. It can be used skillfully or unskillfully. We can get better at it the more we know about its purpose. We can also hurt ourselves if we try to use it for something it wasn't designed to do.

I can drive a screw into a piece of wood using a hammer, but, in spite of how that may look to an uninformed person, the screw will not function properly. I could also drive a nail into a piece of wood using a screwdriver, but it would take longer and damage the screwdriver. If everything is created, everything has purpose. **Finding the right purpose for things will keep us from breaking them, or breaking ourselves against them.**

Once we've made the leap to purpose, we still have work to do. What kind of Creator do we have? What can we find out about our Creator? Did our Creator give us any instructions about how to use sex? This is the point where most people start to feel a little weird. Are we modern people really going to turn to religion to help us find answers about our sex lives? Well I advise you to remember our alternatives. If there is no Creator, there is no purpose and there are no problems. Go right ahead and drive that nail with a screwdriver until your heart is content. There are no rules, and there are no rights and wrongs.

A Creator means purpose that we didn't create, so there are ways to do things that suit the purposes of the Creator. A Creator means we may have explanations for our attitudes and feelings about sex. We have to search for those explanations and see if the Creator gave us any insights. I won't attempt to write about *all* the "religious" instructions about sex, as I am not qualified to do so. What I will do in the balance of this book is to use the Christian perspective on sex as put forth in the Bible.

This means this book is written as if the Christian God is the Creator and the Bible is a reliable explanation of who He is, what He says, and what He does. I understand that there are other views of who the Creator is, and what he/she says and does. I also know there is plenty of confusion about what the Christian perspective about sex is. If you want to explore other religious views about sex there are sources you can use. What I'm concerned about is that you hear the real Christian view before you decide it is false, or doesn't make sense, or doesn't work. Even if you are already a Christian, this book can help you to navigate in a culture full of sexual misinformation and, as we've already suggested, downright deception.

Opening our lives to the God possibility is scary. If God is real, there is no other person with as much potential to disrupt our lives. There is no bigger elephant. All-powerful. All knowing. All present. From the bedroom to the boardroom, God would not only have something to say, He would have the power to conform us to his wishes. Letting a God into our bar might mean it isn't our bar any more. And worse, depending on what kind of God he is, we could end up as slaves to a tyrant who is only interested in obedience and punishment. It is wise to find out what kind of God might be out there before we open the door.

Chapter Three

SEX IN THE KINGDOM

Adam and his wife were both naked, and they felt no shame.
Gen 2:25

Joy is the serious business of heaven.
C.S. Lewis

Have you ever tried to have a serious talk about sex with anyone? It isn't easy to do. I've had "The Talk" with my kids. It was awkward. I expected it to be. But a class in grad school really opened my eyes to the problem we have communicating about sex.

The class was Human Sexuality. The professor opened his lecture on the first day with an exercise. He divided us into groups and gave each a slip of paper. Each slip of paper contained either the name of a sexual organ or a sexual activity. The names given were formal, like "intercourse" or "breasts." Each group's task was to brainstorm together and come up with every slang term they could think of for their assigned organ or activity. At the end of the brainstorming session one person in each group was nominated to stand up in front of the class and read the list out loud.

Everyone in the class was a "grown up" who signed up for it. All of us were serious enough students to be working on advanced degrees. This was not a bunch of middle school boys in a locker room or girls in a bathroom. The exercise lasted about an hour and from beginning to end it was full of awkward laughter, the kind of laughing that comes out of all us when we are nervous. It's the laughter that said, "Can you believe we are saying these things out loud??!!"

The point of the exercise, the professor told us after we all settled down, was to prepare us as counselors for clients who would use terms to describe things in ways we had never heard before, and to desensitize us so we wouldn't laugh when they talked about their sexual problems.

It is awkward to talk about sex. If you find yourself rolling your eyes and saying, "Oh my gosh!" while reading this chapter, it's ok. What is not ok is to let false ideas about sex and Christianity remain unchallenged. God has a positive view of sex. He created it. He made it pleasurable. Orgasms were God's idea. We don't have to infer this from observing creation. We have the Bible.

The Bible is incredibly explicit about sex. Christians who have honestly tried to read and understand the Bible don't come away from it believing God is a prude when it comes to sex. In fact the idea that sex is bad or the body is bad is an infection of Christian doctrine. It was ancient Greek schools of philosophy, which taught that the spirit was pure, and the body (and thus all bodily acts) were impure. This is not Christian doctrine. You won't find this anywhere in the Bible.

The Christian view of sex is this: it should be *both* pleasurable and productive; it should be fun and it should build life, not only physically, but spiritually. No honest reading of the scriptures can leave the impression that sex is a necessary evil, only useful for giving us babies.

Lets have "the talk" from the biblical perspective. We will start with something mild just to warm up. In Proverbs Chapter 5 a father is giving a warning to his son about the dangers of adultery. He explains what adultery will do to him and then says this:

> Drink water from your own cistern, running water
> from your own well. Should your springs overflow
> in the streets, your streams of water in the public
> squares? Let them be yours alone, never to be

shared with strangers. May your fountain be
blessed, and may you rejoice in the wife of your
youth. A loving doe, a graceful deer—may her
breasts satisfy you always, may you ever be
intoxicated with her love.

Obviously the father is contrasting adulterous sexual relationships
with marital sexual relationships. He isn't just saying his son should
sleep with his wife out of duty. He tells his son to rejoice in his wife.
The fountain is a poetic image of desire. He says his son should be
satisfied with his wife's breasts, not in the sense of saying "that's
good enough" but in the sense of really fully satisfying himself with
them and with her. Notice that this has nothing to do with making
babies; it is purely fun, purely pleasure. And he tells his son to be
intoxicated with her love, a clear exhortation to lose himself in having
sex with his wife; to plunge in and drink it in like wine. Sounds like
fun. Sex in God's kingdom is fun, not just functional.

The Song of Solomon is where the fun gets explained in detail. The
Song is an erotic poem that has given translators fits because it goes
further than most of them think proper. I warn you, basically every
body part and every sex act I talked about in my Human Sexuality
class is mentioned in the Song of Solomon. And while those acts and
body parts are wrapped in poetry, they are still pretty explicit. I don't
want to make this an exhaustive study of the Song of Solomon, and
I'm not trying to be a "shock jock," but it is important we hear the
real biblical view of sex. If the Christian God is the Creator of sex,
becoming undeceived about it and learning to use it right means
finding out what He really has to say about it. Here is a sample of
teaching from the Song of Solomon Chapter 7. The man lovingly
describes his wife's body:

1 How beautiful your sandaled feet,
   O prince's daughter!
Your graceful legs are like jewels,
   the work of an artist's hands.

2 Your navel is a rounded goblet
 that never lacks blended wine.
Your waist is a mound of wheat
 encircled by lilies.

3 Your breasts are like two fawns,
 like twin fawns of a gazelle.

4 Your neck is like an ivory tower.
Your eyes are the pools of Heshbon
 by the gate of Bath Rabbim.
Your nose is like the tower of Lebanon
 looking toward Damascus.

5 Your head crowns you like Mount Carmel.
 Your hair is like royal tapestry;
 the king is held captive by it's tresses.

Now he shifts to describing what he wants to do with his beautiful lover:

6 How beautiful you are and how pleasing,
 my love, with your delights!

7 Your stature is like that of the palm,
 and your breasts like clusters of fruit.

8 I said, "I will climb the palm tree;
 I will take hold of it's fruit."
May your breasts be like clusters of grapes on the vine,
 the fragrance of your breath like apples,

9   and your mouth like the best wine.
May the wine go straight to my beloved,
 flowing gently over lips and teeth.

The woman responds to her husband's desire and invites him to come and enjoy her love:

10 I belong to my beloved,
and his desire is for me.

11 Come, my beloved, let us go to the countryside,
let us spend the night in the villages.

12 Let us go early to the vineyards
to see if the vines have budded,
if their blossoms have opened,
and if the pomegranates are in bloom—
there I will give you my love.

13 The mandrakes send out their fragrance,
and at our door is every delicacy,
both new and old,
that I have stored up for you, my beloved.

Wow! What do we find here? Understanding the flow of this poetry is helpful. It is formatted as a call and response between husband and wife. Throughout this passage they take turns admiring each other and expressing their desire for one another. In this case the husband is speaking from verse 1 until the second line of verse 9 where the wife begins to respond: "may the wine go straight to my lover. Obviously he is interested in her body from the tips of her toes to the top of her head and describes both what he sees and what he wants to do with her. He wants to be wrapped up in her long hair (vs5), he wants to take hold of her breasts (vs8), he wants to taste her mouth (vs9). What we miss at a first reading is the progression of his description of her body. Starting at her feet and moving to her head, there is a discontinuity in verse 2 where he describes her navel and then her waist.

Two things are wrong with this translation of this verse; first no one's navel is below their waist and second it makes no sense to speak of a navel that "never lacks for blended wine." The metaphor doesn't work. What does it mean? The husband's hungry gaze at his wife's body is not lingering on her navel. He is describing his wife's vagina. It is next in line in his progressive description of her from foot to head. This gives a double meaning to verse 9. She is not just wanting to share the wine of her mouth with her husband; this is a strong allusion to oral sex. (And yes, if you are wondering if there is an equivalent allusion to oral sex with the partners reversed, it is in Chapter 2 verse 3 of the Song.)

Finally, back in Chapter 7, we have the wife planning an outdoor sexual getaway (vs12), which is not just interesting for it's liberating view of enjoying sex outside in an adventurous way, but also for the freedom the woman has in initiating sex with her husband.

This is the Bible. This is God's Word. This is what Christianity believes the Creator of sex thinks about sex. Sex in the Kingdom of God is unapologetically hot. You will notice there is no mention of the biological necessity for sex and procreation in these verses. Of course God is not silent about procreation. He told the first people He created to 'be fruitful and multiply." I am not trying to avoid reproduction as part of sexuality, but there seems to be more misunderstanding about the Creator's other uses of sex than there is about making babies. In other words most people assume Christianity has little to say about the pleasure of sex and much to say about its productivity.

When you think about it, the Christian God demonstrated that he didn't need us to create people for him; he could literally build people out of dirt. If the God of the Bible created sex and speaks of it in the ways we just read, we must conclude that He isn't just interested in people making more people. God is interested in people experiencing pleasure, and sex is one way He wants that to happen.

Sex in God's kingdom is actually designed for pleasure in it's own right. This is great news. It means we can shed a lot of the guilt associated with pleasure for it's own sake. Sex without reproduction is not a "guilty pleasure," but God sanctioned fun. I know that is not a problem for most people in our culture, but it can be helpful if you were raised with a sexually repressed mindset. It is also helpful for people facing infertility. It means that the inability to produce offspring does not mean we are not "getting it right." In God's kingdom there are legitimate purposes for sex that don't include having babies at all.

Sex in the kingdom is pleasurable. And sex without the kingdom is pleasurable. So what is the difference? If all we want is good sex, who cares how we get it? The problem is illustrated in a story about Iguazu Falls in Brazil.

A boy went on a field trip with his school to visit the falls. Once his class got to the fall, the boy walked up as close as he could get to the rushing waters. He took out a jar, reached out into the foamy water and, filling it up, quickly capped it. When he came home his mother asked him about the trip.

"What was it like, son?" she said.

"It was amazing. It was thunder. It filled up everything I could see and hear." he said. "It was so amazing that I took this jar with me and I reached it into the foam and water coming down the falls and filled it up for you."

As he said this he reached in his backpack, pulled out the jar and, setting it on the table, unscrewed the cap. When nothing happened, he seemed perplexed.

"What's the matter?" His mother asked.

"I think it died!" He said.

The boy expected the falls to be in the jar. The majesty and the roar and the foam. But anything removed from its source is never the same. It dies.

Sex has a source. Pulled apart from its source it may still be pleasurable, like the water from the falls was still wet, but the real power and majesty is gone. The pleasure we have in sex, as in all the pleasures we are given to explore in this life, are not meant to satisfy us, but to create in us a hunger for ultimate joy; full pleasure.

While sex in God's kingdom is created for both fun and functionality, neither of those things is the end of the story. After all, we know that the physical pleasure of sex is not the end of the story either. Do you know people who consistently try to experience the physical pleasure of sex apart from the other pleasures it offers (emotional well being, relational closeness, etc.)? Do those people seem happy or well adjusted to you? There is pretty strong evidence, especially among women, that amassing sexual partners (presumably for the pleasure of sex) without entering committed relationships leads to the polar opposite of pleasure; it leads to depression. And while men don't have the negative emotional results women have, it doesn't mean they are not damaged by pursuing sex for its own sake.

Trying to enjoy sex without God is like trying to get nutrition from food that we chew up but never swallow. The taste of sex is very compelling to us, but without the substance behind it, we are in danger of starving to death with a good taste in our mouths.

God's kingdom has an explanation for both the relational/emotional aspects of sex as well as connecting sex to its ultimate meaning and purpose. Sex in God's kingdom is a pleasure pointing to more pleasure; permanent pleasure, eternal well being; physical, emotional, and relational fulfillment In a sense, without a God-centered view of sex, there is no connection to it's full purpose, it's full majesty, and ultimately it's full joy.

When we investigate sex as a created thing, rather than mere biology, we discover the Christian God is not prudish about sex. The Christian God is too hot to handle for some of His followers when it comes to explicitly pleasurable sex. The God possibility adds meaning to sex that cannot exist without God. Opening the door to this kind of God does not mean sex is diminished in its pleasurability or it's meaning, the opposite is true.

Maybe that is enough to convince us to open the door, but probably not. Why? Because we know there's a catch. The Christian God invented sex, made it pleasurable and fills it with meaning, but He also restricts it to marriage. Why would God give us this good gift and then put restrictions on it? Is this a cosmic bait and switch? Some kind of cruel joke? Can there be any good reason to keep sex confined? Most people think not, but in keeping with the premise that we might be deceived by sex, lets take a look at some facts and see what we find.

Chapter Four

SEX IN A BOX?

*When Joe and I started seeing each other, we wanted
exactly the same thing. We wanted to live together, but
we didn't want to get married because every time anyone
we knew got married, it ruined their relationship. They
practically never had sex again. It's true, it's one of the
secrets that no one ever tells you.*

Sally - *When Harry Met Sally*

*Each man should have sexual relations with his own
wife, and each woman with her own husband. The
husband should fulfill his marital duty to his wife, and
likewise the wife to her husband. The wife does not have
authority over her own body but yields it to her husband.
In the same way, the husband does not have authority
over his own body but yields it to his wife. Do not
deprive each other except perhaps by mutual consent and
for a time, so that you may devote yourselves to prayer.*

St Paul's 1st Letter to the Corinthians 7:2-5

Most people get married. Marriage is still important to us. Surprising
isn't it? It should be. The way marriage is portrayed in most movies
and television shows you would think it was a disease. Statistically we
know a potential marriage only has a coin flip chance of success. But
people are getting married at the same rate as they always have.
Marriage is still what most of us want.

Christianity has a lot to say about marriage. Many, if not most,
people who don't give God or the Bible a second thought, become

interested in both when they get serious about getting married. They want a pastor to do the wedding service. They want Bible passages about love and respect read. They want prayers prayed over them. They want to walk the aisle in a church. What they don't want is God or the Bible in their bedroom. They don't want them there before their wedding day and they don't want them there afterward.

To say the Christian teaching about the relationship between sex and marriage is unpopular is like saying a fox is unpopular in a henhouse. The Bible calls for absolute abstinence from sex outside of marriage and absolute monogamy within marriage. No sex with anyone we aren't married to, and only sex with the person we marry.

The Christian teaching is that sex works best in one context and that context is a lifelong committed relationship between a man and a woman. Most people do not put this into practice. Christians don't *and* non-Christians don't. We generally have sex outside of marriage. This is so "normal" that suggesting we hold off on having sex until we get married seems silly. It is ridiculed. It is old fashioned, outdated, stuffy and impractical.

Our grandparents had a saying about sex and marriage: "if you give the milk away, no one will ever want to buy the cow," meaning sex before marriage damaged your chances of having someone commit to you in marriage. Today we have another saying about sex and marriage: "who buys a car without giving it a test drive?" And most of us do. Today we give away the milk. Today very few people get married without going for a test drive.

Here is a question few people are willing to ask: how's that working out for us? The divorce rate is holding steady at 50% and the divorce rate among couples who live together before marriage is higher than 50%. What could be going wrong with our marriages? Could it be the misuse of sex? Before you discount this as unlikely consider a few things. As the divorce rate began to spike in the late 1960's and into the 1970's several factors tracked along with it. Since the sexual revolution when we supposedly threw off the tyranny of the Judeo-Christian sexual ethic of sex confined to marriage, every measurable statistic about sex shows that more people are having more sex with more people out of wedlock. During the same time frame, the rate of couples cohabitating more than doubled. As many as 60% - 70% of couples now live together before marriage. That means there has never been a time in our country's history when as many people are regularly having sex outside of marriage. At the outset of the sexual revolution of the 1960's, the divorce rate was about 20%, afterward (by the end of the 70's) it was 50%.

Think about that a minute. Do you know anyone who went through a divorce and enjoyed it? Have you ever hung out with a couple who planned for divorce while they were planning their wedding? No. Divorce is not enjoyable and none of us plan on getting divorced.

The situation is this: 90% of us are going to get married in our lifetimes. How many people are sexually "test driving" before they get married? If 60-70% are living together before they get married it would be safe to say that it is indeed a rare couple that hasn't had sex before marriage. And half of our marriages are going to end in divorce.

It was Einstein who said the definition of insanity is doing the same thing over and over again and expecting a different result. Yet that is what we are doing. No one wants to point the finger at sex. Sex is like a slick politician who gets good press no matter what they do. It gets the benefit of the doubt to the point of ridiculousness. Go back to where we started. How much sex is too much sex? Who wants to put limits on sex? If you want to be branded a kook, a radical or just a plain old fashioned bad guy, suggest that sex should be curtailed in any way, that will make you an instant villain, out to stop the great party everyone is having. The dirty little secret is that sex is lying to us, selling us a bill of goods, and ruining our most cherished relationships. The party isn't so great!

Do you want to get married and stay married? Are you already married and want to have a better marriage? Maybe you need to put sex on the stand and cross-examine it. What if the misuse of sex really is the culprit? What if it is breaking us in ways we don't see? It is obvious something is going wrong. No one has come up with a solution to this problem for over 40 years! Is it reasonable to reconsider our attitudes towards sex and marriage? I know it isn't easy to do. It is hard looking along a different line than the line everyone else takes, but it might lead you to discover something great.

One of my hobbies is searching for fossil shark teeth along the James River. The place I hunt is where the river erodes cliffs containing fossils. The cliffs are about twenty yards back from the beach at the river's edge. Walking where the water washes along the shore was the first place I found shark teeth years ago. I learned that when the teeth were wet they had a particular color and shine that made them stand out. It is easier to find them in the surf line. But shark teeth eroding out of the cliffs and into the water get beat up, chipped and dulled, and the really big teeth get broken.

All of the nice shark teeth I've ever found were away from the beach closer to the cliff face. Up there, near the cliffs, the fossils and shells are closer together and there is no water wetting them. It is harder to see the shark teeth and it takes more time, but I've actually found more teeth and better ones near the cliff. Still, every time I go shark tooth hunting I have to fight the urge to walk along the water. I know where the bigger and better thing is, but sometimes the lure of the smaller, easier thing is too much.

When it comes to sex the problem is that most of us think the smaller, easier thing is the ONLY thing. There is nothing bigger and better. And if we don't really believe there is something bigger and better, it is next to impossible to convince anyone to spend the time and energy looking in a different spot.

Years ago walking my beach at the water's edge I came across a broken piece of a megalodon shark tooth. Megs are the largest fossil shark teeth in the world and can measure up to 7 or 8 inches in length. A meg is the holy grail of shark tooth hunting. It is what we hope to find every time we go hunting. That piece of a meg haunted me. I never found anything like it before. It was the very tip of the tooth – the pointed business end - so I could not be absolutely sure it was really a meg. I took it home and compared it to all the other teeth I found at my beach in the past. It had a completely unique geometry. I imagined what the full tooth would look like and decided it had to be part of a meg. From that point on I knew there were megalodon teeth to be found at my beach, but where?

After a few more years of searching where I'd always searched at the edge of the water, without finding even a hint of a meg, I began to consider a new plan. The megs must be eroding out of the cliff face like all the other fossils did, eventually washing down into the water. But they must be too fragile to stay in one piece. They got chewed to nothing by the wash. I needed to find them before they got to the water. I needed to find them close to the point they first washed out of the cliffs.

I moved away from the beach and started searching near the cliff face, convinced there must be whole megalodons there. Every time I went to my beach I fought the urge to search where the sure thing could be found. My time shark tooth hunting is limited. I always want something to show for the effort, even a tiny little shark tooth is still worth finding to me. But I had a piece of evidence to help me; I had a piece of a meg., so I persevered, and kept to my new search pattern near the cliff. It took some time. I left the beach pretty frustrated some days. Some days I doubted I would find my meg, or that there were really any megs to find. But I did find one. Then another and another. Not only did I find my meg, I found other shark teeth larger and in better shape than anything I'd ever found!

There is something better when it comes to sex and marriage. The clues are there in the broken pieces you've seen, and there is a surprising amount of research pointing to just how broken our sexual practices are. Regnerus and Uecker in *Premarital Sex in America* give a prime example of how we miss the truth in their interview with a young woman named Megan:

> She captures what very many young men and women believe to be a liability of marriage: the end of good sex. The last omnibus sex study of Americans—issued in 1994—disputes Megan's conclusion, as do our interviews with married emerging adults. But *the power of surveys and statistics are nothing compared to the strength of a compelling story* in the minds of so many people. We asked Megan whether married life would be less sexual than her single life:
>
> [Do you look at marriage and married sex as being like, "That's off in the future; it might be a disappointment. Now I'm having a better time"?] Yeah. [Do you?] Yes. [Why?] Why do I think it might be a disappointment? [Sure.] Um, just because of the horror stories of getting married. Nobody wants to have sex anymore. [Where do you hear these stories?] Movies, other people. . . . [Like what? Can you think of one?] Um, there's plenty. Like the movie that just came out—License to Wed —there's this one scene where the guy is sitting on top of a roof with his best friend talking about how his wife doesn't want to have sex anymore.

The 1994 study referred to was done by researchers at the University of Chicago, and it was the most extensive study done on American sexuality up to that time. They found that by any significant measure, married partners had both more sex and more satisfying sex than non-married people. More recent studies have not shown any difference. The data tells a plain story; sex inside marriage is not diminished in either its frequency or its enjoyment. But the facts haven't stopped us from churning out sitcoms and movies perpetuating the myth of the sex-dead marriage. It's going to take some courage and faith to believe this, but Christianity offers us the best chance of finding what we are looking for.

The Bible teaches sex in the context of marriage. This can't be because God is trying to limit the amount of sex we have or because God wants to keep our sex lives lukewarm. We've already seen what the Bible has to say about sex and pleasure. The Bible *commands* husbands and wives to have sex – and not just to make babies. So why does God restrict sex to marriage? Is it a restriction at all?

If the Christian worldview is right, humans are not just physical beings who have spiritual experiences, we are spiritual beings who are having a physical experience. How does this affect our view of what we do with our bodies and marriages? We can get a hint by looking at this exchange between some religious people and Jesus. Creating a hypothetical story of a woman who marries seven men, each of whom dies on her, these Pharisees are attempting to trap Jesus into a statement about the nature of the spiritual world. In his answer Jesus reveals something about the nature of marriage:

> But Jesus answered them, "You are wrong, because you know neither the Scriptures nor the power of God. For in the resurrection they neither marry nor are given in marriage, but are like angels in heaven. And as for the resurrection of the dead, have you not read what was said to you by God: 'I am the God of Abraham, and the God of Isaac, and the God of Jacob'? He is not God of the dead, but of the living." And when the crowd heard it, they were astonished at his teaching. (Mt 22: 29-33 ESV)

I have attended a lot of weddings with many different kinds of officiants. One of the weirdest was a wedding on a beach. The woman presiding got a license to marry people through an online ordination. She never mentioned God in the service, but she did talk about the power of love, and how this couple would love each other forever and be together forever like the eternal ocean. It was all very earthy and pleasant and uplifting and also utterly meaningless.

We are not going to love each other forever because we are not wearing forever suits. We are going to wear out. The ocean is going to wear out too. And the sky and the sand and everything else. If we get 85 years it is a good long life. If we get married at the current average age of thirty, and if we manage to keep it going and die on the same day, we can be married 55 years. That is a fact.

The Christian view of marriage is this: we get to be married to each other for 50+ years, but we can be married to Jesus for eternity. If we accept *that* point of view, sex and marriage must have different purposes than we think, or at the very least they must have deeper purposes. We are going to be married beings for a while. We are going to be sexual beings for a while. We are going to be spiritual beings forever. Jesus went to a great deal of trouble, suffering and pain in order to secure our relationship with God and to get us an eternal life; a forever suit. If we put these things together; our spiritual nature and God's rescuing love, we can look at the Bible's teaching about sex and marriage with more clarity. We already know two things God is NOT doing when He restricts sex to marriage:

1. God is not against sexual pleasure, or minimizing the amount of sex people have. We've already looked at this point from one angle, but consider another one; God created marriage and gave us the desire to be married. That would mean God wants more people to have sex, not less.

2. God does not want us to have sex only for reproduction. Song of Solomon alone gives us plenty of evidence that God is pleased with

sexual activity for it's own sake and encourages us to explore his invention to it's fullest.

A God who created sex, marriage, pleasure and people, would not confine sex to marriage in order to cut them down to size. He could have done that from the start. He could have invented it all to run differently. So why did God put sex in a box? Maybe he didn't. Maybe God telling us to keep sex in marriage isn't a restriction at all, but a description of how his creation operates. Maybe there is no box.

In the Christian worldview, sex is not a separate entity as many view it and use it. Sex is an integral part of marriage. Marriage without sex is incomplete and sex without marriage is incomplete. The authentic understanding of sex and marriage isn't that God restricts sex to marriage, but that, He created marriage, which includes sex, and if we pull them apart, we damage both in the process. The evidence for this is pretty strong when we consider the negative statistics about divorce, but it is also pretty strong when researchers study sex within marriage.

As we've already noted, married couples have more sex and more satisfying sex than single people. Another finding of that same study is that cohabitating couples have as much sex as marrieds, but they are less sexually satisfied. Does that sound right to you? If you asked a bunch of college students who are "sexually liberated" (like Megan), and who don't have the hang ups of old married people: "who do you think is having more and better sex, you or your parents?" They would probably laugh at the question, but they aren't the ones experiencing the highest sexual satisfaction or having the most sex.

If you want to take this one step further and really blow those college student's minds, ask them who is having more and better sex, church people or non-church people? Again, by every measure (and by a significant margin) churched people, especially those who have a evangelical religious affiliation, report higher sexual satisfaction.

Here is another piece of data – maybe another piece pointing us to the existence of a meg.

This is what we would expect to find if we are created beings of the Christian God. We would expect, based upon this God's teachings, that people who embrace his ways would have more and better sex. The Christian gospel gives us a place to stand and an angle to look at sex that doesn't exist in other worldviews. It lets us look straight at sex. The beauty of the gospel perspective on sex is that it doesn't condemn sex or try to lessen its importance. The gospel actually lifts sex into a different plane, recognizes its power while at the same time keeping that power in check. If we let the gospel change our perspective, we can actually enjoy sex more because we see it isn't the MOST IMPORTANT thing in the world. We can both take it seriously *and* laugh at it. We can take it seriously because it has God-design and God-value. We can laugh at it because when we see sex parading around as if it is the source of all life and happiness – making outrageous promises it cannot possibly keep - we see it like a badly dressed used car salesman insisting his lemon of a car is the best thing since sliced bread.

You may be right at the door now, ready to take a chance of opening it. There is one last step you should take toward the door. Take a look at those ridiculous promises sex makes; look at what sex is trying to sell you and what it delivers. Is it a good deal?

Chapter Five

SEX SELLS. SHOULD WE BUY?

When I get that feelin' I want sexual healing.
- Marvin Gaye

Or do you not know that the unrighteous will not inherit the kingdom of God? Do not be deceived: neither the sexually immoral, nor idolaters, nor adulterers, nor men who practice homosexuality, nor thieves, nor the greedy, nor drunkards, nor revilers, nor swindlers will inherit the kingdom of God. And such were some of you. But you were washed, you were sanctified, you were justified in the name of the Lord Jesus Christ and by the Spirit of our God.
St Paul's 1ˢᵗ Letter to the Corinthians 6:9-11

It is a common saying, so common we hardly pay attention to it anymore; sex sells. We understand this to mean sex can be used to sell things by association. A quick glance at television commercials shows us sexual imagery associated with cars, soap, and kitchen appliances. The magazines lining the check out aisle at Wal-Mart all include some reference to sex. Sex is selling a lot more than cars, soap, appliances, and copies of magazines. The things sex promises to give us are more foundational to every human being than anything we can buy in Wal-Mart, and this is the reason it is such a powerful additive to any advertising campaign.

The passage out of Paul's letter to the church at Corinth shows us what sex is selling, and it gives us a warning. The warning is in verse 9: Do not be deceived. We started with the question of whether or not sex is deceiving us. Here the Bible clearly tells us that the things in this list have the potential to deceive us and sex is center stage.

Do you know the difference between a lie and a deception? A lie is a direct contradiction of the truth. You ask a child, "Did you eat all the Oreos?" and they say, "No," when in fact they did eat all the Oreos and still have the evidence on their face written in black and white Oreo crumbs. This is a lie. A deception is a lie wrapped in truth; a set of true statements meant to lead us away from a central truth.

While lies are basically power plays (he said – she said), deceptions are subtle manipulations. The story of the powder and the elephant is a story about deception. Imagine how the powder salesman approached the barkeep. What was his pitch? It might sound like this:

Salesman: Can you imagine what would happen if an elephant ran through this place? It would be a mess. (true)

Barkeep: It sure would.

Salesman: It would certainly tear up the place. It might even hurt or kill one of your customers. (true)

Barkeep: That would be awful.

Salesman: I think a responsible barkeep should do everything in their power to keep their customers safe. (true)

Barkeep: Of course they should.

Salesman: What are you doing to make sure no elephants come into your bar?

Barkeep: Well, I'm not doing anything.

Salesman: Don't you think you should protect your bar?

Barkeep: Certainly. Do you know how I could do that?

Salesman: Well, I do have some powder that I've kept in my own home for years and we've never had a problem with elephants. (true)

Barkeep: Do you think it would work here?

Salesman: I don't see why not. It's the same powder here as it is at my house. (true)

Barkeep: I guess I need to get some of that powder.

Salesman: I happen to have some right here if you'd like to try it out. And if it works I can keep a regular supply coming to you.

Barkeep: Thanks. You are really helping me out!

Of course the powder is useless and has nothing to do with elephants, but the salesman has only made true statements. *Not everything true leads to the truth.*

Deceptions are designed to take us away from the truth. The word translated as "deceived" in Paul's words above comes from a Greek word meaning "to cause to wander." If you've ever been lost you know how uncomfortable it feels and how disorienting it is to be really and truly lost. Being deceived is being lost without knowing you are lost.

One of the reasons it is so hard to help people become undeceived is that it is often more comfortable to remain blissfully ignorant than it is to accept the facts and feel the discomfort that goes along with admitting we are lost. It's no fun to become undeceived. It really is like bringing an elephant into your bar.

The Matrix is a movie that shows the power of deception. All the main characters have been "rescued" from the matrix – a digital world where they are enslaved by machines. But the real world (introduced by the man who rescues them as "the desert of the real") is not pretty at all. It is dark and dreary and dangerous. Waking up from the matrix and knowing the truth affects different characters in

47

different ways. Some dedicate their lives to rescuing others from the lie they've believed; but one character is so unhappy with reality that he is willing to betray his friends if only he can go back to his old, deceived life. He can't find anything good about reality in comparison with the lie he lived in the past.

Fortunately, the Bible doesn't just point out our deception, it doesn't just dump us in the "desert of the real," it also points the way to the truth and the way to life. But first we have to let the elephant in. Letting in the elephant involves a simple yet difficult first step: we have to admit that it is possible we are deceived.

Paul tells the Corinthians "Do not be deceived," and gives them a list of things that have the potential to deceive them. The top of the list is sexual immorality. What does he mean? There are a few things we need to understand about the definition of sexual immorality. First, are we biology or are we created? If there is no Creator there is no such thing as sexual immorality because there is no created purpose for sex. Sexual immorality, as the Bible talks about it, is any form of sex that distorts or misuses sex outside of it's created purposes. Again, if we use a screwdriver to hammer in a nail, we aren't using it right even if the end result looks OK to us. We are committing screwdriver immorality, or hammer immorality. You get the point. Immorality refers to taking something the Creator made to do one thing and using it to do something else. Immorality only makes sense in light of morality; and morality only makes sense in light of a real standard that we didn't make up for ourselves.

The second thing about the phrase "sexual immorality" is the scope of it's meaning. In the original language it is a junk drawer word meant to gather up any and all forms of misusing sex. The word is pornos, where we get our word pornography, and, amazingly enough if we follow that word back to it's roots in ancient Greek, it comes from a word that means to export for sale. The core meaning of sexually immorality is an exchange of money or value for sex. Sex really is tied up in the business of making sales and has been for a long long time. What does the Bible have to say about what sex is selling?

In Bible passage above we see three things that happened to people who discovered their sexual deception, and then became undeceived through an interaction with truth. The text says "you were washed, you were sanctified, you were justified." These three things are the true and deeper needs sex claims to give us, and why it has such power over us. We want them all. We need them. Washing, sanctifying, and justification. Sexual immorality, at its core, is trying to get these things from sex when sex is not able to give them. The deception comes because sex is good at imitating these things and delivering a taste of each.

Sexual Washing

For many years in India a strict caste system has been observed. Castes are basically social groupings that inform people how to interact, what they can do for a living, whom they can marry, etc. It is hierarchical in nature, with one caste occupying the place of highest honor and respect and each respective caste taking it's place under the one above it. Castes are also hereditary; people do not join a caste, they are born into their caste.

The lowest of the low in India are the Untouchables; a segment of the population considered so dirty that they cannot be touched for fear of defiling anyone coming in contact with them. Untouchables live in their own communities, work in the worst jobs, cannot marry anyone who is not an untouchable and are not allowed to participate in community life alongside members of other castes. They are unclean. Everything in their society reminds them that they are dirty.

Imagine yourself in a nasty, heavily used public restroom. Everything you touch makes you feel like you want to wash your hands and use some Purell to boot. If you are an untouchable in India, you are the human equivalent of a public restroom, and anyone coming into contact with you acts accordingly.

What would it be like for an untouchable to have sex? What would that be? To be told all your life you are too dirty to look at, much less touch, and then to have full body contact with another person. To be naked and completely touched. What a radical feeling of washing that would be. How completely cleansing to be that touched!

To one extent or another we all feel unclean. We all feel untouchable. We feel "less than" somehow. This is different for different people, but we all experience it. NFL films did a show recapping a recent Super Bowl. In the show a player recounted how he committed a penalty that cost his team a touchdown at a crucial moment. Years later, this professional athlete who achieved more success in football than most people dream of, was still visibly upset. He spoke of the need for redemption and how he played the rest of the game looking to make up for the mistake he made. What was he saying? He felt dirty! He felt unclean. He felt "less than."

No one escapes this feeling. It comes when we fail a test, or when we get an A- (if we are that person) or when we forget a friend's birthday. It comes when people ignore us or forget us or abuse us. One way or another everyone gets a dose of untouchability.

Having another person touch us sexually – full body contact – tells us for that moment at least – we are completely touchable. We are being declared fully clean when we are fully naked and fully intimate with another person. Marvin Gaye captured this idea in his song "*Sexual Healing*":

> And when I get that feeling
> I want sexual healing
> Sexual healing, oh baby
> Makes me feel so fine
> Helps to relieve my mind

Sexual healing baby, is good for me
Sexual healing is something
that's good for me
Whenever blue teardrops are fallin'
And my emotional stability is leaving me
There is something I can do
I can get on the telephone
and call you up baby
And honey I know you'll be
there to relieve me
The love you give to me will free me
If you don't know the thing
you're dealing
Oh I can tell you, darling, that it's
sexual healing

Sex is a strong antidote for the feeling of being untouchable. It contradicts the voice inside our heads telling us we are dirty failures.

There is a problem with this kind of sexual washing. Maybe you've experienced it. It is this: while you are in the bath of sexual touching you feel clean, but as soon as it's over you no longer feel clean. You may even feel dirty! And many of us would even say that a repeated sexual "scrubbing" in certain contexts leaves us feeling dirtier than when we started.

What happens when the thing we expect to declare us "clean" either leaves us feeling more dirty or only works while we are engaged in the actual act? Sex is a disappointment when it comes to making us truly and permanently clean. The best it gives us is a temporary feeling of being clean. We are only sure we are clean while we are engaged in sex. When it's over, we go back to wondering and feeling like we may or may not be clean, sometimes in mere minutes.

So in the case of the first thing sex is selling us, it promises a cleansing, and it gives a cleansing of a sort, but it fades, or worse it promises us a cleansing and actually dirties us.

Sexual Sanctification

Sanctification is a Bible word that suffers from bad press. It sounds so stuffy. To sanctify simply means to be set apart for a unique purpose. It is recognizing something as unique and special and then treating it that way. All of us want to be uniquely ourselves and we want someone to recognize us for who we are as individuals. This is another thing sex is selling us. Sex holds out the promise of being uniquely valued as an individual.

During sex we are being uniquely and completely set apart from all other people. We hope that in giving ourselves to someone in this way they are looking directly at us and only us, and enjoying who we are.

In the movie Groundhog Day, Phil the weatherman is living the same day over and over again. He sees an attractive woman in a restaurant and, day by day, gathers bits and pieces of information about her with the intention of getting her in bed. Eventually he knows enough about her to convince her he is an old classmate from high school. He invites the woman, Nancy, out on a date that ends in his hotel room. It has been a great date for her. This man seems to know her and want her. They are getting hot and heavy when Phil blurts out "Oh Rita! (the name of Phil's producer)

Nancy: Who is Rita? (sitting up and turning on the light)

Phil: How should I know?

Nancy: What, is this some kind of a one night stand?

Phil: On the contrary. I love you. I've always loved you. In fact, this may seem sudden, but Nancy, will you be my wife?

Nancy: Oh Phil! (falling back into his arms)

Phil: Oh Rita!

Nancy: Nancy!

Phil: Whatever.

Nancy is in bed with Phil because he made her feel unique. None of us has sex with someone as a surrogate unless we are actively participating in prostitution. We engage in sex as individuals with other individuals believing we are unique and they are unique. For this moment, at least, there is no one else in all the world like us and we have someone giving their full attention to us. We are set apart.

But sex falls short on its promises again, and in this case perhaps worse than in the promise of washing us. Even in the best of circumstances when both partners are fully engaged and setting each other apart from everyone else, it only lasts as long as the sexual act. We get a temporary form of sanctification; a moment of being uniquely set apart and valued as an individual. Then it is over. We may not even make it through the act of sex before we realize our partner isn't thinking about us at all. Nancy may have to pretend her partner is really looking at her.

Sex between two people isn't always about two people either. We may find out our sexual partners aren't thinking about us or another person, but only thinking of themselves and only using our bodies to get pleasure.

Perhaps worst of all is when a person we've had sex with and believed was valuing us completely and uniquely, has sex with someone else, leaving us wondering if we were ever unique in the first place. Even when our culture insists we can have "meaningless" sex that should not affect us this way, it still does.

Sex promises recognition of our unique identity but doesn't deliver a permanent solution. Just like its promise to wash us and declare us clean, the sanctification sex tries to sell us is a cheap and temporary form, often leaving us feeling less special and less set apart than if we'd never had sex at all.

Sexual Justification

Justification is the act of being set right. It is being RIGHT. Notice that it is NOT feeling right. It is actually being right. Sex is something we use to make us feel right. Why do you think sex is a way that makes us feel right? Think about it. When people are engaged in sex there is usually not an argument going on is there? We aren't fighting over who is right and who is wrong while we have sex. You don't have a sense of being at odds with anyone or anything while you are having sex. Sex is two people in complete agreement with each other. Sex is two people being right with each other

Here is something I've learned both by being married for a long time and through doing a lot of marriage counseling: A couple that has a satisfying sex life can go many years without knowing the true nature of their relationship. The reason is that in our current culture we start relationships with sex and as long as we keep having sex we believe we are in agreement. We believe we have the same values. We believe we have the same goals. We believe we have the same worldview.

Whenever we discover places we disagree or whenever circumstances create a conflict, we have sex and we wonder what all the fuss was about. Sex generates a feeling of rightness that actually masks our real disagreements. That is all it is though, a feeling. There is not a true state of being right.

If we follow the cultural norm and have sex with someone after we've known them a week, or a month or two, what have we really learned about each other? Probably not much, and the things we do know are fairly superficial. But sex, selling us justification, makes us feel right for each other. People outside the relationship often tell us the problems they see, but the sex justification muffles their voices.

We have serious fights with our partners and consider whether we are "right" for each other, and sex speaks up saying, "oh course you are right for each other, think about the last time you had sex. Wasn't it great?"

This interference with our hearing and seeing can go on for months or years and often it is only broken up when sexual activity is interrupted for a period of time due to health issues, an extended work absence, or even if one partner becomes sexually bored or lazy. Once the physical and emotional rightness of sex is removed from a relationship for long enough, people discover real disagreements. Someone actually has to be right and someone wrong. Sex made us feel right, but that is all it was, a feeling. Substantial "rightness" with each other takes much more work than having sex. Once again sex sells us a temporary solution at best.

The reason this is particularly damaging is the confusion it causes us. With the huge emphasis placed on a satisfying sex life in our culture, the feeling of justification that comes along with great sex would seem like the thing everyone is looking for. When sex does a bait and switch on us, giving us the high of feeling right and then dumping us back where we came from, it is more than a physical let down.

Everyone tells us sex should answer all our questions about our partners and set everything straight. Does that sound like a stretch? Think about how our media portray the power of sex. In Alice Sebold's best selling book, *The Lovely Bones* (adapted into a movie by the same name), a young girl is brutally raped and murdered. Her killer hides her body in a field, and she narrates the story as a spirit who observes as her family deals with her disappearance. The girl goes to a sort of heaven while still remaining near happenings on earth. At the finale' of the story the girl, Susie, inhabits the body of her best friend, Ruth and she makes love to Ruth's boyfriend. This act sets Susie free and allows her to let go of earth and fully enter heaven.

Talk about power! Talk about setting things right! Sex overcomes rape and murder. Sex sets things right that even heaven can't cure. This idea of completion through sex threads it's way into most of our popular stories. Is it any wonder we are so devastated when we come up against the fact that sex can't make things right?

Review

So what does sex promise us and what do we get? It promises us washing and we get a spit bath. It promises us full sanctification and we get one Kodak moment. It promises us justification and we get stuck on a feeling.

Is this what we should buy? It doesn't make sense does it? But most of us keep on buying it even after we get burned multiple times. Why do we keep doing this? Two reasons. First is what we've already noted several times. Call it peer pressure or cultural pressure, either way we have to overcome a tremendous amount of "common sense" bombarding us with advertisements touting the greatness of sex. With so many positive messages coming at us, it takes a lot of courage to reject the sex sales job. It is much more common for us to think something is wrong with us, or our sexual partners than it is to think sex itself is falling short.

The second reason is this: none of us wants to live dirty, ordinary, less than right lives. The drive to feel washed, sanctified, and justified is so strong we won't stop pursuing these things. We can't stop. Sex isn't the only way we pursue these things, but it is the most popular and the most widely touted as their source. It is no wonder sex wreaks havoc in us. Is there an alternative source of the three things we need?

The Bible passage we started this chapter with answers that question.

Sex makes claims and Christianity makes counter-claims. The people in Corinth were just like us. Sex wasn't selling anything different when Paul wrote his letter. They looked for washing and sanctifying and justifying in sex too. But we see a group of Corinthians addressed here like this: "you were washed, you were sanctified, you were justified in the name of the Lord Jesus Christ and by the Spirit of our God." "Were" in this context refers to a past event that has continuing consequences. In other words the Bible is saying that these people received the three things we want and they are going to keep them forever. Permanent washing. Permanent Sanctifying. Permanent Justification.

How did this happen to them? The Bible says it was in the name of the Lord Jesus and by the Spirit of our God. This is shorthand for the gospel of Jesus Christ. This is what Christians have called the "good news" since the church began. In fact the word gospel means good news. The claim of the gospel is that it is better than sex.

Sex sells us short but the gospel gives us what we want and need, and gives it to us permanently. I know it sounds outrageous or perhaps irreligious to say the gospel is better than sex. What do they have to do with each other? Everything. I warned you that elephants in your bar are messy. Get ready for a holy mess.

Chapter Six

THE GOSPEL ELEPHANT

Sally: Well, if you must know, it was because he was very jealous, and I had these days of the week underpants.
Harry: Ehhhh. I'm sorry. I need the judges ruling on this. "Days of the weeks underpants"?
Sally: Yes. They had the days of the week on them, and I thought they were sort of funny. And then one day Sheldon says to me, "You never wear Sunday." It was all suspicious. Where was Sunday? Where had I left Sunday? And I told him, and he didn't believe me.
Harry: What?
Sally: They don't make Sunday.
Harry: Why not?
Sally: Because of God.
- When Harry Met Sally

For your Maker is your husband—
the Lord Almighty is his name—
the Holy One of Israel is your Redeemer;
he is called the God of all the earth.
- Isaiah 54: 5

I'm going to use a bit of a graphic metaphor. It may be a bit disturbing to some of us, but it is biblical. Here it is: through the gospel, God is offering to take you as his lover. This is difficult to accept at first, but it is a metaphor God uses throughout the Bible.

The Bible teaches that God comes to all of us with an offer of marriage. He loves us. He is fully available to us. God proposes to us. God accepts anyone who accepts his proposal. He promises to be their bridegroom. Those who come to him are called his bride, the church. The gospel is both personal and corporate. Each member of the church is a bride and part of the bride. Keeping with the metaphor, a Christian is a person that God marries and takes as a lover.

God comes into full contact with us. The passage in the letter to the Corinthians we looked at in the last chapter says those who came to God were washed, were sanctified, and were justified in the name of Jesus. He gives us his name just as a bridegroom gives his name to his bride. God comes into full body contact with us through the Holy Spirit entering us. Is that too graphic? Christianity isn't for the squeamish. It isn't dainty, and it doesn't look away from the full ugliness of sin or the full implications of grace. The gospel is real or it isn't. It is true or it isn't. The premise of our culture is that whatever works for you must be true, but Christianity only works for you if it is true.

Before you decide the gospel isn't real or true, make sure you know what the gospel is and what it is not. The gospel is God doing everything necessary to be spiritually united to those who accept him. It isn't a set of rules to keep in order to keep God happy with us or to carry out until we are pretty enough for him to consider marrying us. The gospel is a marriage proposal from the most beautiful, interesting, accomplished, smart person in the universe to you; an unconditional proposal to you, just as you are.

What if the gospel really is true? What would it mean for us? Lets go back through the three things sex sells us and look at them in the way the Bible tells us they are given to us in Christ.

Gospel Washing

Obviously God doesn't need to be washed. He is clean. God is completely other than we are. Holy. Complete. We are not. The feeling we have of needing to be washed comes from being less than holy. We are not complete. This feeling never goes away. After every success we feel it creep in again. After every washing, sexual or otherwise, we still sense it. We fail by our own standards. We don't feel whole. Talk about untouchables! We are the untouchables. We are the lowest caste.

But, in the gospel, God comes and says through Jesus Christ – I will touch you; if you let me I will make you my own treasured possession. The Gospel is a permanent cleansing because the Holy Spirit enters the believer and takes up residence never to leave us or forsake us (Hebrews 13:5). When our own hearts condemn us; when we fail by our own standards; when we feel dirty, we have something greater than our last lover or our next lover to look to, we have a Spirit of complete clean-ness living inside of us, and God's opinion that trumps any other opinion, even our own:

> This then is how we know that we belong to the truth, and how we set our hearts at rest in his presence whenever our hearts condemn us. For God is greater than our hearts, and he knows everything. (1 John 3:19-20

The kind of washing God gives us through the gospel is a permanent solution to feeling dirty. Since we do not earn the presence of the Holy Spirit through keeping the 10 commandments, or reading the Bible, or doing good deeds, we can't lose it by failure to do those things.

The reason the gospel is really good news is that we don't earn any of the benefits of being in a relationship with God. He gives himself to us freely from the start and knows what he is getting into when he proposes to us. It's not as if God is going to wake up one day and try to sneak out of our lives like a lover who is embarrassed to find themselves in bed with someone like us. See what the Bible says: *he knows everything!* Does this sound like the way we think of our earthly lovers? Don't we hope they never see everything? Don't we fear that if our lover really saw everything; all the ugly, dirty things about us, they might not stick around??

God knows us completely and sees us clearly and chooses to get in bed with us anyway. God is the most clean person in the universe and he comes into full person-to-person contact with us through his Spirit. This is the ultimate declaration of being clean. We may feel dirty at times; we may hear voices in our heads calling us unclean, or failures, or unacceptable, but the Holy Spirit is there to contradict those voices, and the story of the gospel stands in front of us to show us what God was willing to do for us in order to be in a relationship with us.

There was a critical point in the history of the church when the story of God's work through Jesus Christ had not passed beyond the boundaries of Israel. Jesus was a Jew and all his followers were Jewish. These followers did not set out to tell non-Jews about the gospel. To the Jews, all non-Jews (called "Gentiles") were like the untouchables of India to the higher castes.

Peter, a close follower of Jesus and leader in the new church, had a dream. In his dream God told him to kill and eat "unclean" animals. Peter refused to do it, saying, "I have never eaten anything common or unclean." God replies, "what I have made clean, do not call common." The next day Peter, the ultra-clean Jew, finds himself in a home full of Gentiles - which for a Jew would be the equivalent of entering a public toilet in Times Square.

We can see the implications of the gospel and the previous day's vision click into Peter's brain as he says to this gathering of Gentiles:

"You yourselves know how unlawful it is for a Jew to associate with or to visit anyone of another nation, but God has shown me that I should not call any person common or unclean." (Acts 10:28)

It is God's opinion that matters. What He calls clean is clean.

Gospel Sanctification

Not only does God cleanse us, but the gospel is also God setting us apart. The gospel isn't that Jesus died for the sins of the world. Jesus died for us as individuals. It isn't just a blanket covering of what's broken in the world. It's a specific individual effort to come to you.

God our lover stays with us and helps us to become fully ourselves. He teaches, leads and delights in us. Because no one can know us like God knows us, no one sees our potential like God does. No one knows how utterly unique we are, and no one has the resources to help us become fully ourselves.

One of the ugliest misconceptions about Christianity surrounds the idea of sanctification. We hear the word and think of stuffed up, puffed up, self-important people who don't do anything wrong, so they don't do anything except judge people who do. *Sanctimonious is not sanctified.* God doesn't set us apart to keep us apart. God doesn't set us apart to pull us apart.

If the gospel story is true, God, the most glorious, powerful and free being in the universe, confined himself to a human body for over 30 years, and died a horrible death on a cross in order to get a relationship with us. He did this so we could know him and he could know us in a relationship of love, not power. The point is, God could force anyone to conform to anything he desired and no one could resist. If God sanctifies us it must be understood in the context of the gospel; in the context of a lover who has the best interests of their lover in mind at all times.

God proves through the gospel He is willing to go to any length to see us become our full selves. Sanctification isn't God making us into something unrecognizable, it is God making us into what we really are. It is the disposal of all our distorted visions of who we are supposed to be while we embrace a truer and higher and more full self. Our Guide is not taking us there to make us into a trophy wife at the end of the process. God doesn't need us to make him look good. C. S. Lewis, writing in *Mere Christianity* puts it best:

> The more we get what we now call "ourselves" out of the way and let Him take us over, the more truly ourselves we become. There is so much of Him that millions and millions of "little Christs," all different, will still be too few to express Him fully. He made them all. He invented—as an author invents characters in a novel—all the different [people] that you and I were intended to be. In that sense our real selves are all waiting for us in Him. It is no good trying to "be myself" without Him. The more I resist Him and try to live on my own, the more I become dominated by my own heredity and upbringing and surroundings and natural desires. In fact what I so proudly call "Myself" becomes merely the meeting place for trains of events which I never started and which I cannot stop. What I call "My wishes" become merely the desires thrown up by my physical organism or pumped into me by other men's thoughts or even suggested to me by devils...

Remember what sex was selling? You are unique! (for the moment) You are special to me! (right now) No one wants you as much as I do! (until this act is over)

God the lover demonstrates utter commitment to you and has the ultimate ability and knowledge to fulfill you as an individual. And God has nothing to gain from it. Sex, outside its God-context, will never be attached to a partner who isn't looking to get something from us – to "become" something by sleeping with us. God is already fully himself. He isn't trying to get something from us; he is trying to help us become our true selves. Gospel sanctifying means getting and keeping a unique identity that not only won't be taken away, it is going to grow into the full you.

Gospel Justification

The gospel makes us right. If you notice the left margin of this book, you see that each line of text starts at the same place relative to the edge of the page. The text is "justified." Everything takes its place relative to an agreed upon spot. It makes the document readable. It helps make the document make sense. Most of us never think about justification when we read. We open a book or click on a web page to read a blog and expect the text to line up. We would only notice it if

the text

          didn't

  line up

                       and it started

to

       annoy

                                    us.

Sexual justification gives us the feeling of being right but it doesn't make us right. Sexual justification lets us line up our lives against something momentarily. It is true that it is hard to feel wrong while we are in the throes of sex. Two people are "right for each other" at least as long as their sex life is regular and satisfying, but without the sex, justification fades. The margins aren't set. It is like having a document where anyone can randomly go into the settings and change the margins.

Without God there is no Right thing. There is no way to know what a crooked line is unless you see a straight one. God is the straight line. To come into alignment with God is to be made right, not just to feel right. It isn't a mask, it is the real thing. You can push up against it. It won't move. It is sure. He is sure. Lovers move. Both lovers move. During the very act of sex both partners are changing physically, mentally, emotionally, even if it is only in small barely noticeable increments.

God is the lover that never moves. The Bible says Jesus Christ is the same yesterday, today and forever (Hebrews 13:8) and that in God the Father there is no variation or shifting shadow (James 1:17). The justification of the gospel brings us into line with the real margin of the universe. We can always know who we are because we have a permanent relationship with a God who doesn't change his mind about us or move away from us regardless of what we do. We are not lined up with Him because of performance or effort. He came and did all the work for us to make us right with him. Gospel justification, like gospel washing and gospel sanctification, is a permanent gift for anyone willing to believe and accept the marriage proposal of the God who moved heaven and earth to be with us.

A person who accepts God's proposal of marriage and becomes God's lover is not slammed up against the righteousness of God. God doesn't treat those who come to him as perpetrators of evil who are handcuffed and marched up against an unyielding wall. The gospel is this: whatever spaces there are between us and God's true straight line margin, he fills up with love so compelling that it draws his lovers to himself. In the gospel we are actually made right (justified) before we try to become right. And we are kept right (justified) whether we feel like it or not. The washing and sanctifying and justifying of the gospel are all like this. God does the work through Jesus Christ, consummates his relationship with all who come to him through giving his "lovers" the Holy Spirit, and then patiently and persistently helps his them walk into their new identity.

The Holy Mess

Now the gospel elephant is all the way into the bar. We can see what it looks like. What did it step on in your life? Did it break a chair or two, things you thought were worth sitting on? Or did it shake the whole counter and break all the glass? No doubt it is a large animal. The gospel makes large claims. The gospel makes claims that are outrageous and hard to ignore. If you let this into your life it will make a holy mess of things. But tell the truth; how clean was your life before you opened the door? Was everything really so tidy and neat? Isn't it true that opening the door and letting the sunlight in shows how shabby the furniture was to begin with?

The real difference between gospel people and non-gospel people isn't the mess; it's only whether it's a holy mess or just a mess. Remember the quote from the letter Paul wrote to the people in Corinth? He wasn't writing it because their lives were perfectly set in order. He was writing it to remind them about the gospel as the way to keep cleaning up their messy lives - and if you read the whole letter you will see the Corinthians were a messy bunch.

We may think we live in an overly sexualized culture, but even with the internet and cable TV we have nothing on Corinth. In the ancient world to "Corinthian-ize" meant to live a lewd, sexually promiscuous lifestyle. Corinth was an ancient version of Vegas. Male and female prostitutes were a normal part of temple worship. In other words sex was openly used and acknowledged as the way to get washed, sanctified and justified. Everyone did it and accepted it as normal. This was the context into which the gospel first came with its claims. This is where the gospel elephant showed up. Do you think it disrupted people's sex lives? It certainly did. The gospel restructured their lives – their whole lives not just their sex lives. It put sex in a different place than it had been before the gospel came to them, but that doesn't mean the gospel put sex down or made it ugly.

The gospel doesn't claim sex isn't important, nor does the gospel try to put sex in a corner as a "dirty little secret", as many people seem to think Christianity teaches. What the Bible does teach is that sex is a tool that can be abused by people who don't understand the gospel and is best used by people who do understand the gospel. What the Bible claims for the gospel; the more penetrating cleansing, the more complete recognition of personhood, the more perfect perfecting of identity, and the more permanence of it's effect, means that sex isn't what we need to have a great or full life; Jesus is.

This is a crucial truth regarding sex. It gives us room to breath in a sexually breathless culture. It takes away the urgency to jump into bed with someone so we can have a life. It means we can be better lovers because we are not entering sexual relationships for selfish reasons. When we consider what the Bible teaches about sex being part of marriage we can know it isn't a restriction of our joy if we aren't married, or even if we never get married. If the gospel is God being available as lover to anyone, no one is left out of the real essence of sex; the deeper promises that it is designed to reveal.

What if you are already married? Are you safe from sexual deception? Is a wedding ring a "magic bullet" to protect us from sexual distortions? And what does the gospel do to help you stay undeceived once you get married?

Chapter Seven

MARRIED WITH ELEPHANTS

The man and his wife were naked and they felt no shame.
- Genesis 2:25

*Maybe if we think and wish and hope
and pray it might come true
Baby then there wouldn't be a single thing
we couldn't do
We could be married
And then we'd be happy
Wouldn't it Be Nice?* - The Beach Boys

A young man asked to come see me in my office one day. He was obviously distraught. He was a Christian. He believed the gospel. He knew about gospel washing and sanctifying and justifying. He also knew the biblical teaching about sex and marriage. He followed the Bible teaching about sex from his youth. He was a virgin.

The problem he had was that he started dating a girl, fell in love with her and asked her to marry him. She wanted to marry him, but she said that meant he must know her sexual history. He was crushed to find out that she was not a virgin. He asked me what he should do. He said he always imagined that being true to the biblical teaching meant God would give him a spouse who would do the same. Finding out his potential wife had had sex with someone else made him think she might not be "the one."

There are plenty of holes in his thinking, but in light of the gospel, can you see the biggest? He was obeying the Bible instruction about sex and marriage, but he was hoping to get a wife out of it who could make him feel special. That is why he was distraught. The gospel sanctifying was not enough for him. God himself dying on a cross for him was not enough to make him feel set apart. He needed a woman who never had sex with any other man to make him feel set apart.

This was not gospel based thinking about the woman he loved. What was it? It was sex lying to him about what it could do for him and what he should expect out of it. And he bought it. Fortunately this young man could still hear the truth about the gospel - the gospel elephant could still walk in and rearrange his mental furniture. He changed his mind about his girlfriend's sexual history and his own. He saw both as belonging to God and available for God to use to glorify himself and to grow both him and his future wife.

The promises sex makes us don't go away when we get married, and they don't go away if we abstain from sex outside of marriage. The promises sex makes us distort our ideas about what sex should do for us. If we waited to have sex before we got married, it doesn't mean we aren't deceived about sex, it may only mean we bought into the lie that sex within marriage will wash us, sanctify us, and justify us. If we participated in sex before marriage, we got washed, sanctified and justified under false pretenses, and we may not be prepared for sex to operate properly in our lives. It is possible for marriage to amplify sex's lies.

My wife and I worked part time for a catering company for years, and so we have been present to see the first moments of hundreds of marriages. We also see the behind the scenes work of couples trying to create their weddings.

It is incredible to see the effort that goes into a wedding these days. The average American wedding cost $25,000 in 2012. That is a lot of money. It is interesting to note that as divorce rates began to rise in the 1970's, the amount of money spent on weddings rose exponentially. In other words as the chances our marriages were going to fail increased from about 2 in 10 to 1 in 2, we started spending astronomically more money to launch the wedding ship. The more lavish the weddings, the more pressure to get everything just right, and the more expectation that everything will be all right "ever after," especially sex.

If you just spent half a year's salary to get married, what should the sex be like after that? It should be spectacular right? If it is the first time or the thousandth time it should be amazing. And then, if it is spectacular and amazing knock-your-socks-off sex, where do you go from there? If you believe sex is going to make you feel washed, special, and right, you have to believe married sex is going to do those things better and longer. When it doesn't you are going to start asking hard questions about yourself and your spouse. Without the gospel, your answers will fall short.

The gospel is the full answer. If we keep the gospel in the center of our lives it depressurizes the bedroom, which can lead to increasingly satisfying sex. Two people who know that God has called them clean, and special, and right, are able to enter into sex and marriage with much more freedom than anyone who looks to get those things from another person.

This doesn't mean people who know the gospel never struggle with sex in their marriages. The Bible recognizes how hard it is for us to navigate marriage and sex even when we know the gospel. The biblical teaching provides two essential elements to keep sex in its proper place. They don't sound "sexy" but they work together with the gospel to set us up for an authentically satisfying sex life. The elements are security and discipline.

Security

A few years ago I was having lunch with a friend in a downtown Norfolk cafe. It was an outstanding late summer day. Sunshine. Clear skies. I sat leaning my back against the plate glass window front, near the street. The glass began to rattle. I thought it must be a large truck coming down the street. When it continued to increase in intensity and no truck appeared, I realized something strange was happening. It was an earthquake. I know that some people out West don't think much of a little 5.8 Richter scale ground shaking that lasted mere moments, but earthquakes don't happen in Virginia. Everyone jumped on their cell phones and checked up on loved ones. It was the lead story for all the local TV news stations that sent their reporters out to get stories of water sloshing out of people's back yard pools (no lie, that was really on the news). Why was there so much fuss? Things moved that were NEVER supposed to move. Suddenly everyone in Virginia realized that Virginia itself could move. It was unsettling to say the least.

When I do pre-marital counseling, I ask every couple if they are having sex. As you can imagine, the vast majority are. When they say "yes," I ask them why. Inevitably the answer is something about being in love and being committed to each other. When I press in on this I find that they have decided to have sex because they "feel" it is right for them. It is a mutual decision based on their feelings for each other.

There are problems with this. Marriage is a long relationship. Many things are going to change. Spouses are not always full of the energy needed to have sex. Seasons of sexual drought come to every couple. Childbirth and children interrupt our rhythms. Our bodies change. What was "normal" for us at 25 will not be normal when we are 40, or 75.

Another question I ask every couple is this: how long do you want to be married? This often brings a strange look between the two and then back at me. Usually they say, we want to be married forever. Good answer. No one gets married expecting to give it a few years and then leave each other.

Why are those two questions so important? Even in our super liberal sexual climate, I've never heard anyone suggest they'd like to have their spouse sleep with someone else, yet if we project ourselves a few years down the road and apply our pre-marital standards for when sexual activity is permitted, we are asking for trouble.

When your husband has become sexually disinterested, why shouldn't you have sex with the nice man at the office who is attractive and pays attention to you? When your wife doesn't act like she loves you any more and isn't looking as attractive as she used to, why not have sex with the perky aerobics instructor at the gym who looks good and acts like you're worth spending time with?

We expect to stay married forever and we expect the person we marry to be sexually faithful. By setting our own standards of sexually acceptable behavior based upon our feelings, we set ourselves up for conflict. Most people who have affairs are just being consistent in their belief systems; in their single days they felt it was ok to have sex with each other, and one day, for whatever reason, they felt it was ok to have sex with someone else and so they did. Consistent.

Applying God's instructions about sex and marriage gives us security. God's instructions aren't going to change. We can agree they are our standards no matter what our circumstances may be. This gives consistency to our sex ethic and builds security into our marriages. No earthquake will move God's sex ethic. Two people who agree that God's instructions about sex are correct have a security that others only think they have, but can disappear in an instant even after years in a seemingly secure relationship.

God's instruction is not just a guarantee to keep us from sleeping around, however. Security is the key element for growth. The

Christian teaching that sex and marriage are part of one thing doesn't mean that getting married automatically makes us sexually capable. Sex in marriage is more like muscles in our bodies. We can learn to work specific muscles to build them up and improve our strength and endurance, but we can also neglect our muscles and become weaker.

The truth is that sex is not really graceful and airbrushed, it is awkward. No two bodies fit together the exact same way every time we try to fit them together. Part of the beauty of gospel-secured sexuality is the ability it gives to us to laugh at the incongruities involved in sex. It isn't the end of the world if we make a mess out of it. Our core identities are still intact.

Knowing we are held together by God and not our sex lives actually gives us the freedom to be more sexually adventurous; to risk looking silly, or to admit when something didn't work. The Bible doesn't just tells us to stay true to each other, though, it insists that we practice our sexuality together.

Discipline

Discipline?? Yes. Christianity provides a framework for regular sexual activity between husband and wife.

Years ago when I first read the Bible I came across this passage in 1 Corinthians:

> The husband should fulfill his marital duty to his wife, and likewise the wife to her husband. The wife does not have authority over her own body but yields it to her husband. In the same way, the husband does not have authority over his own body but yields it to his wife.

I was pretty excited about this part of the Bible. In fact I called my pastor, got him on the phone and said, "This is about sex right? This means my wife needs to have sex with me whenever I ask her to, right?" I barely let the poor man speak. All I wanted to hear was a "yes," and I hung up the phone so I could go find my wife and have a Bible study about these two verses.

OK that was a bit silly on my part (and it didn't work out exactly the way I planned it), but the point is that within marriage God provides for ongoing sexual *work*. If marriage and sex are what God tells us; an invention that works as one thing, two people who get married are going to learn to use sex better than anyone who uses sex outside the context of marriage. But that doesn't mean it is simply going to happen. Sex may happen, but great sex never just happens.

One of the most damaging myths loose in the world today is that sex is easy and everyone should be good at it naturally. It's as if we are all born with sexual skill like a dolphin is born swimming. In the sexual template of our time, red-hot sex is only possible if it comes naturally and in a burst of inspired passion. This is patently false. It takes work to get good at anything. It also takes time. Sex is hard. It isn't intuitive. The boys in the locker room lie to each other about how good it is and how good they are at it. The girls paint rosy pictures for each other about their experiences.

Getting married doesn't solve sexual problems. Because of our cultural sexual mythology, it often creates problems. Sex takes work and God tells us that sexual laziness is not an option. The security created by God's sexual ethic to only have sex within our marriages is not a license to goof off, it is securing space for us to practice sex with each other in all it's awkwardness. A place where failure isn't fatal and we have the time to explore our sexuality without fear or pressure; but we still have to do the work. Having God's instruction to keep working on our sex lives doesn't give us more energy at the end of a long day or make us feel more attractive when we aren't at our ideal weight, but it does give us something more than our feelings to motivate us. You may not believe it before you get married, or as a young married person, but sexual "chemistry" doesn't get it after a while. We need more motivation to keep having sex and to get better at it.

The Bible addresses the most common sexual problem we will face in marriage; a mismatch in desire for sex. Perhaps no other area is so full of stereotypes in our culture than this. Men always want to have sex, right?. They wake up thinking about sex and go to bed thinking about it more. Men can be up to their eyeballs in work one minute and ready to get in bed the next. Men need no foreplay or afterglow. Women are hard to get into bed. Women would rather hold hands. Woman need a long time to warm up and a decent amount of time to cool back down. Women want to make love, not just have sex.

Most of these ideas are continually reinforced through our media, and, as in all stereotypes, have some basis in reality, but none are THE TRUTH. Many women are confused when their husbands are not as interested in sex as they are. Some find a slow down in their mate's sexual activity as ominous; they begin to think pornography or another woman must be to blame. Men who can't keep up with the sexual demands of their wives are embarrassed and think they must be defective.

The truth is that we are male and female, but we are also emotional, physical, and spiritual beings, and uniquely unique. The desire to have sex with each other is something every couple will deal with on a regular basis. We are all moving targets with certain levels of energy affected by environmental factors beyond our control. There is no "normal" amount of sex in a relationship according to the Bible, there is only an instruction to remain sexually available to our mates on a regular basis. If we agree that God's teaching is our guide, we will be able to work through the many changes life brings by looking to use our bodies to serve our spouse, not just to meet our own needs. This discipline of mutual submission to one another sexually is a practical expression of what a gospel marriage is aiming for: mutual submission of all our lives to each other.

Fear the Elephant

The true and better discipline of marriage is actually found in a much misunderstood and misquoted part of the Bible in Ephesians Chapter 5:

> Wives, submit to your own husbands, as to the Lord. For the husband is the head of the wife even as Christ is the head of the church, his body, and is himself it's Savior. Now as the church submits to Christ, so also wives should submit in everything to their husbands.

> Husbands, love your wives, as Christ loved the church and gave himself up for her, that he might sanctify her, having cleansed her by the washing of water with the word, so that he might present the church to himself in splendor, without spot or wrinkle or any such thing, that she might be holy and without blemish.

This appears to be the formula for being married as a Christian. Wives submitting to husbands and husbands loving their wives. But this is not really how it works. We do not have the ability to look at our spouses and submit to them, sexually or otherwise. This leaves us open to deception. When our wives are not lovely and our husbands are not respectable, how can we keep on going? Especially in the bedroom where we feel so vulnerable and...naked! The real discipline of Christian marriage is in the verse that is usually left out of the quote above. It is in the verse just prior to this passage:

submitting to one another out of reverence for Christ.

The key to a Christian marriage, and therefore to a Christian sex life, is the continuing reminder that we live with a huge elephant in the room. In the boardroom, in the living room, and in the bedroom.

We don't submit to our spouse first. We don't look at our spouse first to see how we should act. We look at Christ first. We see in the Christian gospel that Christ was willing to get dirty, to lose his special place, and to become wrong (the Bible actually says that Jesus Christ became sin, which is to say he became not just wrong, but assumed all the wrong that ever was in the world – 2 Corinthians 5:21); Jesus submitted himself to all of that so that we could be washed, special, and right.

Christian marriage and sexuality operates in an environment of "reverence for Christ." In some translations of the Bible this is rendered "fear for Christ." What does this mean?

I grew up out in the country in a house that was over a hundred years old. There were several barns standing on the property which fell into disrepair. One of the barns evidently served as a trash dump because underneath it there was a pile of refuse which had accumulated over years and years. The dump fascinated me. Everything in it was from the early 1900's. It was my own personal archeological dig site and I spent hours excavating it and collecting antique cans, bottles and assorted junk. But one day as I dug a trench into the pile I opened a hole. A huge black snake came out of the hole like a jack-in-the-box.

That was the end of my dig site. Every time I thought of going back down into the barn I thought of that snake. The snake became my primary reference point when it came to that barn, and it still is to this day.

This is what it means to "fear" Christ. Not that we are afraid he will pop out of a hole in the ground and bite us, or scare us, but that who he is, what he did and what he said will be our primary point of reference no matter where we go or what we do. No matter how long we live and how long we are married the gospel elephant is not going to move. We will always know it is there; He is there, and because of who He is and what He did for us we will always be able to see how washed, and special, and right we really are.

Sex has been lying to us for a long time and is not going to stop. No sex, great sex, wait for sex, married sex, the gospel will be there to remind us of who we are. None of us are sex objects no matter how loudly our culture screams it at us. We are subjects of the Creator, made to enjoy Him and in Him to enjoy each other.

Chapter Eight

NO GOD, NO GLORY

Whoa, this is heavy.
- Marty McFly

*Mount Sinai was covered with smoke, because the Lord descended on it in
fire. The smoke billowed up from it like smoke from a furnace, and the
whole mountain trembled violently.*
Exodus 19:18

I wrote this book for people who grew up in our highly sexualized
culture; people who believe some or all of the 10 myths of chapter
one. I wrote it because, as I said earlier, more than 90% of us still
want to get married, in spite of the 50-50 chance of divorce. I wrote
in the hope you will read this book and get free from lies that hurt
you and lead you away from full life. And I mean a full life, not just
a full sex life or a great marriage. Jesus said the whole reason he
came was for us to have this:

> The thief comes only to steal and kill and destroy; I
> have come that they may have life, and have it to the
> full. (John 10:10)

The word for "life" used in the original language is the Greek word
"zoe." It is the root of our word "zoo." It is a word meaning life in
all its aspects; in all its expressions. When is the last time you visited a
zoo and took in all the life?!

If you are like most people, when you decide to get married, you look for a church to hold the ceremony and a (priest, pastor, preacher, minister) to conduct it. What's that all about? You want God involved in your wedding. It brings some weight to the whole thing, right? You could go to city hall and be legally married in a few minutes with no preparation at all. You could get married in your backyard with the lady who got her license to marry people off the internet and bought a robe at a thrift store. But most of us don't. Why? It doesn't feel right. It feels too lightweight and none of us wants a lightweight marriage. We want marriages that endure. We want to go the distance. Adding a God element makes sense. God will always be God; if He's anything, He's heavy.

The Bible has a word for this; glory. Glory means weighty. When the Bible says God is glorious it is telling us that no one or nothing has more weight than God. We can get an idea of this from the account of God coming down on Mount Sinai in the book of Exodus. The whole mountain shook. God is more glorious than a mountain. He is more real. He is more permanent. He is more durable. If we want anything in our lives to be permanent, it is our marriages. I've never met a person who plans to be married less than a lifetime. We want glorious marriages, so we invite God to our weddings.

I end up working with couples who want me to invite God to their wedding ceremony, even if they don't know him personally or they've ignored Him for most of their lives. They are surprised when I ask them if they are having sex. The look in their eyes says "Of course we are, nobody would be stupid enough to get married without making sure everything works in bed" or "Of course we are, we love each other, and we aren't going to listen to you tell us it's wrong for us to express our love this way." We want God to come to the wedding and it would be nice if He would help us stay married, but we don't want Him in our bedroom before the wedding and we generally want Him to leave us alone after the ceremony, maybe even before the reception, because, you know, He's kind of a buzz kill…

The problem with this kind of thinking is that God doesn't have a saltshaker full of glory to use on us. God's glory isn't pixie dust. God's glory doesn't exist apart from God, it is not even part of God. God is glory. God is reality. C.S. Lewis put it this way in his essay *The Weight of Glory*:

> If you want to get warm you must stand near the fire: if you want to be wet you must get into the water. If you want joy, power, peace, eternal life, you must get close to, or even into, the thing that has them. They are not a sort of prizes which God could, if He chose, just hand out to anyone. They are a great fountain of energy and beauty spurting up at the very center of reality. If you are close to it, the spray will wet you: if you are not, you will remain dry. Once a man is united to God, how could he not live forever? Once a man is separated from God, what can he do but wither and die?

Where God is, there is life and health and reality and permanence; where He is absent, all those things are absent, and the best we can do is nothing more than an echo of eternity.

I tell couples who come to me, asking me to invite God to their weddings, that I am willing to do it, but only if they are willing to invite God into our counseling sessions and into their bedrooms. I ask them to stop having sex until they are married. I don't do this because the statistics tell me this improves their odds of a longer lasting marriage, although this is true. I do it because it is a tangible way of acknowledging God's glory – God's presence – in an important part of their lives.

We've been over this once, but it bears repeating. Please listen up. I know you love each other. I know sex makes you feel closer. I know you think you can set your own limits and rules about sex. But you aren't thinking past the end of your own nose. You may have had quite a few sexual partners in the past for various reason, but when it comes to your marriage partner you are having sex because you feel love and commitment in the act. You feel it is right.

Remember our discussion about "right-ness"? If you set the edges of right and wrong then they are only as permanent and real as you feel they are. Marriage is a long run, not a sprint. There are things coming that will push your feelings out of shape. There are times of sexual drought coming because of work, children, illness, and other circumstances. There are times when your partner is not going to look or act as attractively as they do today. There are going to be people who look good and treat you better than your spouse. Those outsiders won't have to deal with the logistics of running a household, paying bills, caring for children, and a hundred other things that take up our energy. They will be sexually available when our spouse is not. Let me tell you one other thing I know; I know that no matter what your sexual history is, you don't want your spouse having sex with the girl at the gym or the man at the office. You don't. And all you have to go on is your feelings. You decided what was right long ago. Now it's up to you to decide it is right to have sex with someone else or to stay faithful to your spouse. It's all on you and your feelings. Not a great plan. Shortsighted. Lightweight.

Mike and Val (not their real names) met in high school and started having sex with each other on a regular basis at 16 or 17 years of age. After high school, they moved in together and set up house. By the time they came to see me about getting married they had been living together for at least 5 years. They wanted me to counsel them about marriage. I'd known them a long time and knew they were aware of God's words regarding sex outside of marriage. They both went to church and said they believed the gospel, but when it came to sex, they didn't get it. They didn't see the big deal.

This was early in my counseling career and it was a challenge to me. This couple functioned well as far as I could see. They had good relationship dynamics and communication skills. They were friends and lovers. What did I have to offer them? I knew what I believed about the gospel and about God's instructions for sex and marriage, but before me was a couple that seemingly "worked" well, in spite of their violation of God's words.

What should I tell a couple like this? It occurred to me that they were asking God to get more involved in their relationship now. Up to this point they ran most aspects of their relationship without consulting God. They were confident they could "get it right" on their own. Now they wanted children, and with great insight, realized how that was going to be a whole new and different ball game. They wanted help. I pointed out the obvious: if God was right about one aspect of their relationship, why wouldn't he be right about all aspects? If they were going to trust him about their future and children, shouldn't they trust him with their present and sex?

This was tough. A couple living in the same home sleeping in the same bed and experiencing the American dream. It was a test for me to tell them what I wanted them to do. Stop having sex. Now. Promise each other, and me, and God you will honor his ways with regards to sex. I told them if they would agree to this I would counsel them and perform their wedding. I told them I thought there was a blessing in it for them. I told them I didn't know what it would be. Perhaps it would be a mountaintop sexual experience compared with years worth of molehill sexual experiences. Maybe they wouldn't notice anything new in bed, but to be sure it would be a blessing because God is not into restricting our freedom, He is into releasing us into the freedoms that suit our nature. I told them to go away and talk it over and get back to me.

At the time I thought one or both of them might resent my request and refuse to work with me, but it only took a day for them to let me know they wanted to work with me and would accept my conditions. I counseled them and married them several months later.

Mike and Val both said their decision turned out better than they could have imagined. They've been married almost ten years now. I wrote Val for this book and asked her how following God's plan worked for them in the long run. This is what she said:

> Mike and I both agree and have told people till this day that it (agreeing to forgo sex until their wedding) was well worth it. I feel it made us closer as a couple. It also gave us time to grow our relationship with Jesus. In a marriage sex is so important, however, it's not everything. I think it is very important for two people to know there is true love, not just lust. I also believe God did bless us for taking that time. Sex after marriage is very different in a very good way. I never felt more connected to Mike than on our wedding night.

This is typical of couples who come to me. No one has ever told me they regretted the decision to invite God into their sex life. I've never had a couple refuse to continue counseling because I asked them to stop having sex. Should any of this be a surprise? I learned something important when I started working with couples looking to get married; once they are alone with me and it's just us talking about their relationship, it filters out all the noise of their surroundings. All the stereotypes and myths about sex and marriage and relationships fall apart when it's just God and us. God is glory. Whenever we get near him we see how much more real He is than our cheap substitutes. It's easy to let go of lies when the truth is not only so clear, but so compelling. We want it. We want glory. When our eyes clear we see the gospel is the giving of glory. It is the only way we could get it; God coming to us, God offering to stay with us; always. Glorious.

Chapter Nine

THE CURE FOR SEXUAL VERTIGO

I finally got to talk to You and I told You just exactly how I felt
Then I held You close to me and kissed You and my heart began to melt
Girl You've got control on me, cuz I'm so dizzy I can't see
I need to call a doctor for some help
- Tommy Roe, *Dizzy*

Every good and perfect gift is from above, coming down from the Father of
the heavenly lights, who does not change like shifting shadows.
Letter of Saint James 1:17

I hate rides that go in circles. I can't take them. Spinning rides are a
sure fire way to ruin a day at the amusement park. I can't even ride
the horses on the carousel, or look at them very long. My wife on
the other hand can ride anything. Well, she used to be able to ride
anything, until she got a spinning overdose.

It happened in a traveling roadside carnival. She got on something
with a name like "The Cyclone" with her dad. The carnie strapped in
a load of folks who paid their 50 cents, cranked up the music, and let
her rip. Then he stepped away to parts unknown and the Cyclone
went on and on and on. Maybe the guy had to use the restroom or
maybe he was smoking something; whatever he was doing the carnie
left the people spinning for well over five minutes. They yelled for it
to stop. People got sick. It went on. Finally the guy came back and
let them off the ride. Tina was messed up in the head. Really. She
had vertigo. Ever blow your nose and the whole world took off
spinning in circles for a minute or two? Vertigo is that for hours on
end.

Years after the ride she still suffered bouts with vertigo. Eventually the attacks were so frequent we decided to see a specialist to try to get rid of it. The treatment was kind of crazy. She went into a dark room where they put a helmet on her and strapped her to a table. The helmet covered her whole face and it flashed a sequence of lights in front of her eyes which she was tracked while the table moved into various positions for set time periods. At one point Tina was hanging upside down in the dark wearing a helmet full of flashing lights. If you told me I was taking my wife to fix her vertigo and this was the cure, I'm not sure what I would have thought. It wasn't even in my mind that this existed. But she walked out of there cured of vertigo. She never had another attack.

When you find out you've been deceived by sex and decide to get off the circus ride, it isn't an easy transition. We've seen how sex puts a spin on relationships. Spin long enough and spinning may feel more natural than not spinning. You've probably seen this at work in some of your friends. They are on the relationship ride with someone who is no good to them, or for them. One day they see it and break up with the shmuck; they get off the ride and they seem better, more themselves, and happier. A week later you talk to them and they are back on the ride with the same person who does the same things that made them sick in the first place. What happened? They've gotten so used to spinning that being still feels bad. They jump back on the ride just to make the disoriented feeling go away.

We've seen how sex affects us even when we are not directly involved in sexual activities. In our culture sex is so big it actually has a gravitational field. It pulls us toward itself and it creates spin. If you've been involved in sexual relationships the pull and the spin are hard to escape even after you realize what sex is doing to you. When it comes time to enter what we hope will be a long term loving and committed relationship, sex still has gravity; it still puts a spin on things. It is likely one or both partners will enter a relationship with an active sexual past, and this can contribute to ongoing sexual dysfunction and deception.

Our sexual past is not insignificant. It is real and it is there. We have to do something with it, and burying it won't work. It is like radioactive waste. Twenty years from now it will be just as toxic as it is today and when it seeps into the groundwater of your life it will hurt you and others. Ignoring or burying our past does nothing about the roots sex puts into our hearts. We will have bouts of sexual vertigo that will make our heads spin. It may not mean we run back and get on the Cyclone, but it will affect our ability to enjoy life to the fullest, including our marriages. Once we see what sex is doing to us; the orbital spin it puts on us, how can we stop the sex spin cycle, get off the ride and keep it from pulling us back in? How do we help others get away from their sexual deception so they can have a full, enjoyable life with real relationships?

Here is an example of how some of us try to deal with sexual vertigo from a recent "Dear Prudence" advice column by Emily Yoffe of Slate

Dear Prudence,

I have been married to my wife for two years, and we've been together for five. We have a great relationship, and both of us consider ourselves incredibly lucky to have found each other. However, **so that I could understand her better**, she recently told me some things about her past that have troubled me quite a bit. She said she has had quite a wild sexual past. She has slept with male strippers, been involved in aggressive sex with multiple partners that involved hitting, slept with a number of married men, cheated in most relationships, enjoyed getting choked during sex, and possibly even shared a sexual partner with her mother. She said she did these things because she was sad and depressed and sex made her feel better. She told me these things not to make me jealous or to hurt me, but for me to understand she is happier since she met me than she ever has been and doesn't need to do these things anymore. I am having a hard time getting these images out of my head. Furthermore, I'm afraid this sounds like sexual addiction and that it could resurface. I'm desperate for advice. (emphasis added)

—Reeling Husband

This man's wife had a wild ride in her sexual past. It's obvious she bought into the deceptiveness of sex and found it was not giving her what it promised. She got off the ride and found a good man. She should just be happy ever after. Reeling Husband says they consider themselves incredibly lucky to be in a great relationship. Why did she decide to tell her husband about her sexual past? If they are so lucky and happy together, why not leave it alone and get on with living the dream? She wanted her husband to understand her better. This is another way of saying she wants her husband to know her completely.

Remember our discussion about expecting sex to make us unique and special? Wild Past Wife is still looking for complete sanctification. She wants to be utterly known, holding nothing back, utterly set apart with her husband. We know we are not set apart completely until all that we are is known completely. What is she doing brining all this up to her husband? She is trying to get over sexual vertigo. She loves her husband, but 5 years of stability has not stopped the spinning in her heart. She knows it. That's why she told her husband.

Her husband, however, is in trouble now. Instead of helping her find stability, he started spinning. He caught her vertigo, and now he's the one going for a ride. So what does he do? He reaches out for expert advice. He seeks higher authority, or at least outside authority. Why? He wants to get an opinion from someone who isn't on the ride. He is looking for stability. He loves his wife and doesn't want to go for a spin. He wants to be solid for her, but it's not that easy. Prudence is outside the ride. Prudence isn't spinning. He hopes Prudence can help to keep them from losing it.

Here is Prudence's answer:

Dear Reeling,

I understand your distress because I'm now trying to get the image of the mother-daughter sex party out of my head. Your wife violated two rules: One, she didn't tell you when she should have told you. Two, when she told you, she told you too much. But you now need to put what you've learned into perspective. You two have been together for five years, and you don't indicate that during that time you have ever had cause to doubt your wife's fidelity or her satisfaction with your sex life. I don't know if meeting you was the turning point in her life, or if by the time she met you she had moved past her emotional problems and was ready for a more fulfilling relationship. Whatever it was, it's clear that when you got together she was a different person from the one who sought out illicit and even degrading encounters. You must know that people do change and that many people are able to leave destructive habits behind for good. Your wife was not obligated to spill all to you when you were courting. But at some point after you two became serious, she should have informed you to some degree about her past, enough to convey the salient point that she once went through a difficult period during which she "self-medicated" through sex. She could have mentioned that she'd slept with married men and been unfaithful in previous relationships without going into detail. It would have allowed you to have a sense of her past without having disturbing images seared in your mind. What's important now is for you to remember that your wife is the same person you've known for the past five years, and that there's no reason this **confession** should cast a shadow on your good fortune at finding each other. It would be sad if her desire to have you understand her better leads to your loving her less. You just recently got this news and have understandably been ruminating on it. Now it's time to stop. See if you can decide to push these thoughts out of your mind and make the choice to return to being grateful for your life together. (emphasis added)

—Prudie

Is this really going to help? The trouble with Prudence is, nice and intelligent though she may be, she has no authority. She is an outsider, but she is no outside *authority*. When she tells Reeling his wife violated two rules, it should occur to him and anyone else to ask, "Whose Two Rules?" When she suggests the wife was obligated to share some parts of her sexual past but not others, we can rightly ask, "Who gets to decide how much sharing is enough, what parts have to be shared, and what parts left out?" When Prudence tells Reeling it's time to stop thinking about his wife's sexual past and see if he can push those thoughts from his mind, we can say "Why?" Prudie is saying, "Relax. Remember how lucky you are and forget about this problem. Don't you know everything is going to be fine?" How does she know everything is going to be fine, and why should Reeling believe her?"

Wild Past Wife and Reeling Husband want help with sexual vertigo and they instinctively do what many of us do. Confession and outside authority are important elements of treating sexual vertigo, but they fall short of the full cure. They can give temporary relief, but we need more comprehensive treatment. So what is the full cure? It will probably sound strange to your ears – something like lighted helmets, dark rooms and titling tables – but it can cure you. It is biblical confession. Biblical confession can heal sexual vertigo. It is the way off the spinning ride and it is the way to treat our hearts for the after-affects of sex. Reeling Husband, Wild Past Wife, and Prudence are on to something the Bible explains in the letter of Saint James:

> And the prayer offered in faith will make the sick person well; the Lord will raise them up. If they have sinned, they will be forgiven. Therefore confess your sins to each other and pray for each other so that you may be healed. The prayer of a righteous person is powerful and effective. (James 5:15-16)

Confess sins to one another and pray. It sounds both easier and harder than it should be. On the one hand there has to be more to it than just saying words that can cure sexual vertigo. On the other hand it doesn't sound enjoyable to say our sins out loud to anyone, especially our sexual sins. How can we know to whom we should confess? How do we know we can get the words right? Why should I go into a dark room, put on a helmet and be strapped to a table? How do I know it will work?

We have to understand what confession is and what it is not in order to answer these questions. Confession is a word many people think they understand, but they don't. It is much deeper than we know because without a God confession loses it's meaning and it's value. That is why I was careful to call this "biblical confession." Biblical confession has three distinct elements and all three must be present for it to work on our hearts. Biblical confession is definite words, with definite people, in a definite context.

Definite Words

The biblical word translated "confession" is homologeo. Homo = same, and logeo = word or idea. Confession is not just saying you did something wrong, nor is it saying you did anything at all. Confession is coming into agreement; being of one mind with God.

Teams have logos. Every player wears the same logo. When players don their jerseys bearing the team logo, they symbolize their unity; their single-mindedness. Remember our discussion about justification? When God tells us his ideas on a subject he is not just giving us suggestions, nor is he giving us restrictions we have to live under. When God expresses his word on any part of life you are hearing the manufacturer's precise instructions on how it works. God's words tell us how things are, not just the way He wants them to be. He exposes the framework of the world; the things that will not move for anyone at any time.

God's word on sleeping with someone else's spouse is "Don't do it." Adultery was out of line when God told Moses on the mountain thousands of years ago and it will be forever. Adultery doesn't work, it tears us up and hurts communities. Why? Because it is out of line with the way God made the world.

In order to confess we have to see the line and say it is right, not just see ourselves and wish we were right. Confessing is aligning ourselves with God's ideas and words. It is taking God's logo and saying we have the same logo. The deeper this goes into your heart the more things stop spinning. Every time you look at the stationary word of God and confess it you are touching something absolutely permanent in the world and countering the effect of all the temporary words and ideas that try to put their spin on you.

Definite People

The "each other" in biblical confession is a specific set of people. Saint James, was writing to people who shared a common faith in Jesus. Jesus was what they held in common, not race, or social status, or gender. When we talk about biblical confession you may have pictured a Roman Catholic image of a priest and a booth where people go to tell their sins to a specific person. This can certainly be biblical confession, but this isn't the only place and person for it.

Confession is with "each other." If we share a common faith in Jesus, I can confess to you and you can confess to me. In fact, the way the scriptures are written strongly implies this is how confession normally works; it is a mutual activity, not a one-way activity.

Some of you probably are thinking, "I don't have to confess my sins to anyone but God." True., there are plenty of places in the Bible telling us to do that, but only once does the Bible associate healing and confession. What is the difference between this mutual confession and confessing to God alone?

Confession to God alone is therapeutic. It does heal our hearts, but lets face it, how risky is it? How concrete is it? Confession to God alone leaves us open to a certain measure of deception. How honest are we? Do we really see where we are out of line with God? Do we really see how much we are out of line with God? We are blind where we are blind. We need help to see where we are deceived and how much it is affecting us. None of us lets the elephant all the way into the bar on our own.

Confession to others is risky, but it is also real. Saying our sins out loud may mean we get rejected, but it may mean we get corrected. This correction works both ways. Some of us don't know how badly out of line we are; others think they are way out of line when they're not. Shame and pride are two blinders stopping us from getting our lives in line. God tells us to confess to each other to get rid of both.

When we confess our sins to others who agree that we have been out of line yet refuse to condemn or reject us, it stops the spinning. Biblical confession happens in a community of people who agree with God's words (logos) and accept each other even when their lives don't line up with those words. Confession proves we can have real

95

relationships. It proves we can show ourselves as we are. Sex will keep trying to spin us around and redefine us. Confession gives us a touchstone of reality to keep us in line with truth and life.

Definite Context

How do we get the courage to say our sins out loud to each other? Seeing we are out of line with God's words and finding other people who agree with God's words doesn't mean we will confess. It is still frightening. We need assurance. We need to know it's going to be ok.

Biblical confession is definite words with definite people but it is also in a definite context. "Pray for one another," is the context. It is crucial for healing vertigo to understand this. In fact, taking any one of these elements out of the confessing equation could create more hurt than healing. Remember Wild Past Wife and Reeling Husband? She used definite words and she involved another person in her confession, but it created more spinning;.

The people we need to hear our confession are not people who agree with us, they are people who agree with God. It is the God context where we find the people to hear our confession. It is the God context where we recognize we are out of line, but it is in that same context where we learn that being out of line isn't fatal. The Bible doesn't say "confess your sins to each other, and judge each other so that you may be healed," nor does the Bible say, "confess your sins to each other and forget about it so that you may be healed."

The God context is prayer; "pray for one another." We are not hearing each other's confessions on our own, we are hearing them together with God. We are not hearing each other's confessions in order to hammer each other back into line, we are hearing them in order to ask God to help us all come into line. Unlike Prudie, God knows exactly where the line is and how out of line we are. He has the authority to call us back into line and the resources to help us get there. When God says everything is going to be all right it isn't idle talk or wishful thinking, it's because he moved heaven and earth to make everything all right. He promises his help to anyone who asks to be made right.

Staying away from the spinning ride is not easy. Sexual imagery is not going away any time soon. Pornographers are going to adopt and adapt new technology to make their industry more realistic, accessible and profitable. People around us who are spinning want us to get on the ride with them. The 10 myths are still in full effect in our culture. It's going to take more than will power to keep from falling back into the lies sex sells. Biblical confession works because the repeated practice of becoming vulnerable with each other before God creates the kind of intimacy we are looking for when we have sex. Confession lets us wash off the feelings of doubt and fear we have in our hearts and replaces them with the feeling of being known and accepted. It is a means of setting our hearts right with God and with other people. Being both a person who confesses and a person who hears confession gives us balance; we don't wobble at feeling we are the only ones in need of help. We both ask for help and give help. The confessing community becomes a steady environment where we know we can escape the spin the non-confessing world tries to put on us.

It can be very intimidating to try confession; especially when it comes to our sexual activities. Many of us have said something like this when it comes to our past actions: " I will never, under any circumstances, speak of this to any other person." You may have believed this for a long time. The thought of revealing it may terrify you. If this is you I want to suggest a few things. First, there is no such thing as involuntary biblical confession. It doesn't exist. No one can make us confess, and no one should insist we confess a particular sin or part of our lives. So relax. Breathe. Second, the Christian gospel is that the God who sees that very thing you most want to forget is not rejecting you because of it and only wants you to be utterly free from it; including the fear of having it exposed.

The Christian God is into freedom. Fear of being known is a form of slavery. It is a cruel form of slavery because it is self-enslavement for life unless we get over it. Finally, your desire to be known completely will not die out, ever. The inner conflict between your desire to be utterly known and your fear of exposure is a vertigo generating engine in your heart that will keep you spinning or using up your precious time and energy trying not to spin forever.

If you've never experienced confession before and you want to try it, listening to others is the best way to start. People who have gone some distance with Jesus are more likely to have developed places where they practice confession. These can be called by many names and come in many forms. Small groups, accountability groups, men's prayer groups, and women's prayer groups are all potential places for hearing confession. If these groups include prayer they usually include confession. Hearing others confess helps form an idea of what it feels like and confidence that you can do it too.

There are also specifically formatted programs, which can guide you through confession. These programs include training for people in prayer and hearing confession. One of the best of these is *The Steps to Freedom in Christ* by Neil Anderson. The normal way of using the Steps is to systematically go through areas of our lives with two people of the same gender, using prepared prayers that name specific sin and God's words about those sins. The Steps include a section on sexual issues that is very thorough and helpful.

If you want to have long lasting healthy relationships you are going to need to learn to practice confession. Biblical confession works. Your heart can be still and happy. You can escape the spin cycle and get over sexual vertigo. It does take courage, but you can be known completely and be completely free. Jesus said it:

> The thief comes only to steal and kill and destroy; I have come that they may have life, and have it to the full.

Postscript

THE ORIGINS OF THE ELEPHANT

This is my first book. I'm not telling you this to soften you up, or to ask you to go easy on a rookie. If we take our precious time to read a book we should expect it to be well written and worth our while; otherwise we should stop reading and find another book. Life is too short to read poorly written books. I'm telling you because the topic of this book was not my idea, and it amuses me that the first effort I release to the public is about sex. A friend read an early draft and messaged me: Sex, sex, sex, that's all you think about! If the stats about how much men think about sex are to be believed there is some merit to her observation. While I am a typical man when it comes to thinking about sex, and while I like to write, writing a book about sex never occurred to me. Even when it finally did, I didn't want to write a book about sex. I'd rather write a novel. I'd rather be the new C.S. Lewis. Why did this one make it out first?

The book happened like this: by chance I encountered a couple "making each other happy" (as my dad used to say) in a school bus parking lot (more about that later). The encounter led to some soul searching about what I should have done or not done. Soul searching led to writing a letter to the anonymous couple coupling in the car (see Appendix A for a copy of the letter). The letter became the basis of a sermon I preached to my church community. One of the church members was a friend who I'd told about my goal of writing a book "one day." That friend is Ted. After I preached the sermon Ted exclaimed, "There's your book!" He was insistent and excited. He didn't have any doubt I should write my sermon into a book. Ted infected me with the confidence that this book was worth doing – a confidence I myself had never been able to attach to any one topic long enough to pursue it to a bookish conclusion.

The same summer I preached that sermon I was doing premarital counseling for a couple from outside my church. The couple told me they were not professing Christians, but wanted me to counsel them any way. They gave me permission to work with them and treat them like I would treat any premarital couple I counseled. I love working with couples, and especially premarital couples. This couple was great fun. They were wide open and willing to share their lives with me.

When I counsel Christian couples I usually tackle sexual issues on the front end. But this couple was different. They were living together, and sexually active, and so what? They had no allegiance to Christ, so why single out sexual issues? Instead we worked through their relationship bit by bit and let the gospel illuminate each area. They showed me an issue, we discussed it, and then I would tell them, "If the gospel is true and you were to accept it personally and believe it, this is how it would impact this issue." When we got around to discussing sex I approached it the same way.

All along I saw light bulbs going off for this couple. When I talked about the gospel and forgiveness, the gospel and communication, the gospel and money, I could see it making sense to them. The gospel and sex produced the same result. I saw them illuminated with the truth. They realized sex didn't produce what it promised to produce; that it is not the source of relationship they and their peers make it out to be. I saw them realize that the gospel was the true source of relationship. When they both decided to personally embrace the gospel, it was as illuminating to me as anything that ever happened to me in ministry. I saw it was effective to lay the gospel down beside the ideas we have about money, and power, and sex, and just let it expose the holes.

When you are trying to write a book critiquing our culture's views about sex you need that kind of encouragement. Sex is the fount of all blessing to us. If you want to make yourself a target, try suggesting any kind of restraint or modification to sexual behavior;

the arrows will find you. This couple gave me hope I could write a book about sex, compare sex to the gospel, and there were people who would be willing to listen what I had to say.

The final piece that pushed me over the finish line was the discovery of a book by Mark Regnerus and Jeremy Uecker, *Premarital Sex in America.* The book is amazing and well written. The more I read the more I saw how their research agreed with the gospel. Their interviews with young people from all over the country include story after story of people who are deceived by the promises sex makes to them and who can't figure out what to do about it. Their sexual practices are tearing up their lives, but they don't (or can't) blame sex! Sex is the one universal good and no one is allowed to question it. Regnerus and Uecker's include a chapter on ten myths young Americans believe about sex and relationships, which convinced me to finish this book. In my business I end up counseling people who are victimized by sexual misconceptions so damaging and so deeply rooted they often cost them their most important relationships. I know at first hand the ten myths are active to one degree or another in couples who come to me for help both before and after they get married, and I'm sure sexual deception hurts our chances at having what we all want: loving, committed, and lasting relationships.

So I wrote this book. My first book. I have a lot of hopes for this book. I don't know who you are or how you ended up reading it. I hope a friend gave it to you and told you it was helpful – those are always the best books no matter what the subject. I hope you will be able to do the same for someone else you know. The gospel came to a community, grew in communities and lives in communities. Good news is always like that; it is only genuinely good if it's good enough to share. I hope you'll see that I wrote this as a friend, for my friends. Most of all I hope you embrace the good news personally and see that the gospel really does deliver on all the promises sex makes to us but fails to keep.

Appendix A

LETTER TO THE COUPLE COUPLING IN THE PARKING LOT

Below is the letter I left on the car of the people having sex in the school bus parking lot. I hope they read it and let the elephant in. I never got a response. I hope you will respond and I hope you will find real glory and real life.

Dear Occupants of (here I wrote the vanity license plate of the car)

Would you take a moment and consider some words of truth and wisdom? I hope so. I really hope I'm not wasting my time and that you both could have a revelation about your self and life.

Being young and being full of hormones is nothing new. All of us go through it. Your parents did, your teachers did, your bosses did. I know it's hard to imagine these "old" people feeling such strong emotions and urges about each other, but they did. You probably think nobody understands what you are going through, but you'd be wrong. Most of us have gone through it.

Here's the interesting part: take a moment to look around at those parents, teachers, and bosses. Look at the adults around you, the ones you can't imagine having the kind of passionate urges that you have, and see the truth. You are going to be them some day. The hormones will settle down. The lust will even out. You will still be passionate, but it will be in different ways with different goals.

There's nothing bad about this. People can't live at a fever pitch their whole lives.

And let me tell you another very important and interesting point: sex is fun, enjoyable, and pleasurable, but it doesn't last very long does it? Moments ending with high sensations and then gone. Gone. No one can live all the time at that height. We have to come back down to earth. Sex is a liar. It promises to give us intimacy with each other, and it does, but only for a moment. It promises to make us feel close and it does, until we part. It promises to make a lasting connection between us, to keep us committed to each other, but it doesn't. You don't even have to look at adults to know this is true; just look around at your classmates who are sleeping together and how long they stay connected. And if you do look at adults you see the divorce rate is 50%. You think all those people didn't feel the way you feel when you're having sex?? Of course they did. It's just common sense to see that it takes more than sex to have a relationship with someone.

Maybe you don't care about relationships. Maybe you're just fooling around; having fun. Maybe. Maybe that's what one of you thinks and the other one does care. I'd bet, if you look into your heart, it's likely both of you do care even if you don't admit it to each other. Regardless let me tell you why it matters what you are doing with your bodies sexually right now.

You were made to be loved and accepted. Some of the ways we try to feel loved and accepted are to achieve with grades or with sports or in a job. People applaud or reward us. They tell us how proud they are of us. This feels like love and acceptance. Sex is a way many of us try to satisfy the desire we all feel to be loved and accepted, after all when we are having sex it's pretty obvious the person we are with accepts us, and we usually believe they love us too. The particular problem with sex as a way to satisfy our needs is that every time we give away physical intimacy without committing our whole selves to another person, we create a false connection that will get ripped away. The more we try to get love and acceptance sexually the more it will disappoint us and leave us feeling empty. It's like what happens to your hands when you do hard work. Over a period of time you build up calluses; places on your hand that no longer feel. The cycle of sex substituted for real intimacy eventually builds up relational calluses; places on your heart that no longer feel. You will find it harder and harder to trust people and believe they really want to know you. It will become harder to know real acceptance and find real love.

You may be one of those couples who say "yes, but we really love each other," "we were made for each other," "we're going to be together forever." This principle is still true for you and will make your life together more difficult. Why have you decided to have sex with each other? Because of your own standards; your own beliefs. This is all you have to stand on. What if one of you decides they love someone else and wants to have sex with them? What then? You have nothing to appeal to; no standard you agree upon, no reason to restrain yourself other than your own belief in each other. There are a lot of things coming in life. A lot of things that are going to make you "feel" differently than you do now. It's a terrible thing to be run by our feelings. They can change in a moment; they can cycle with the weather. You are going to need more than feelings to stay together.

I said earlier that you were made to be loved. Do you realize that is a statement of faith? It is a statement about the nature of the world and about ultimate reality. If we are nothing more than products of electro-chemical chance and processes which began without a plan and play out according to scientific principles, then love is just chemical and happens for no reason. Actually what we call love doesn't exist if we are just well evolved animals. In that case seeing two people going at it in the stadium parking lot is no different than watching a couple of orangutans doing it at the zoo. But if love is real then it had to come from somewhere outside the world. It had to pass from a Creator into creation. There really is no way around that when you think about it. Everyone lives like love is true but few of us take the time to understand what that really means. It means God is real. It means what we do really does matter to him. It means there are ways that are true and ways that are false. Obviously I'm not the kind of person who is out to punish people who disobey God's word. I could have ensured you were caught in the act or I could have reported you to the school after I found your car. Instead I am sitting here writing you this letter and hoping to help you live a better life – a full life even.

I am a Christian. I believe God's word is true. I believe he says sex outside of marriage is wrong. Instead of just saying that, I've tried to show you why that is true; why it makes sense. You see, God isn't simply waiting to hammer us when we do wrong things. God isn't trying to keep us from having fun. Think about this: God invented sex. Does that sound like God is a prude or doesn't want us to have fun? It was His idea! When God tells us to keep sex within the context of a committed covenant relationship (marriage), he is actually telling us this: the best sex ever happens within marriage (this is actually a statistically proven fact) AND having sex outside marriage is going to do us harm. Breaking God's laws doesn't bring God down on us in his wrath so much as breaking God's laws is punishment in itself. It's being stupid. It's hitting our own thumbs with a hammer. God made us and he claims to know how we humans work the best.

Why should we believe him? Why should we miss out on all the "fun" that people are having who break his laws? Where is the guarantee that we aren't being duped? Well I said I was a Christian and I believe that only in Christ can I make the case for you to follow God's laws. If you know the Christian story that God came to earth as a man and died on a cross for the forgiveness of our sins and rose from the grave to demonstrate his power over all our enemies; if you know about the gospel and Jesus Christ, then you know that God was willing to go to any length to set us free from sin. What is sin? It's living like we have to find our own love and acceptance somewhere other than God. Sin comes from an archery word, which meant to "miss the mark" (as when an arrow doesn't hit the bulls eye). None of us can hit the mark every time. All of us miss somewhere. If you believe Jesus is who he said he is, and if you accept His love and acceptance as yours, then you can start to believe that God's laws are not to hold you back from anything, but to release you to live fully.

This has turned out to be a very long letter. I don't know if you will even read it. If I were in your position I think I would be a little shaken up by getting a letter like this, wondering what is going to happen. Well I'm not going to do anything more than this. I've given you the best words I have to give. I've loved you with the truth. I sincerely hope you will not waste these words. You will not always have the opportunity to look at your life clearly and make decisions without coercion.

If you would like to contact me and discuss the matters I've written about, my email address is:

elephantinthebar@gmail.com.

Appendix B

Data and the Social Sciences

Observing our world as it is often leads us to ask questions and to form ideas about why things are the way they are. This is true of physical phenomena (why is the sky blue?) and social phenomena (why are half of marriages ending in divorce?). Once we think on a subject for a while we form opinions about factors we think contribute to a particular phenomenon. This opinion is called a hypothesis. We test a hypothesis by gathering experimental data to see if the results confirm them. If we collect enough data over time that fits a hypothesis we can establish a theory. OK, thanks for the elementary school science refresher, right? But we have to keep the basics in mind when we consider the value of data collected in support of the social sciences. Take note in the next few weeks how many times you read an article or watch a news story having something to do with human behavior that includes the words "a recent study." I'm confident you will find more than one, and the data may in fact be very useful, but use caution accepting what you hear at a face value.

In the social sciences constructing effective experiments that produce completely satisfying results is notoriously difficult. In the hard sciences there is a bias toward finding what the researchers want to find in the data even when the data are quantitative. In social science, the bias is also in the subjects tested. A Hydrogen atom doesn't think about how it acts or about how the scientist observing it feels about how it acts; people do both. Social scientists have to account for tons of variables, and even when they do, people will always be variables. It is not uncommon for researchers in the social sciences to conduct studies that produce seemingly contradictory results. When this happens it doesn't mean the data are wrong in one case and right in the other. It could mean both researchers accurately captured the best data they could given the subjects and conditions of their study. It could also mean one or the other researchers found what they set out to find and missed everything else. The most reliable data comes from studies conducted over a long period of time with a large sampling of subjects. We can see better with a little more distance what the trends in our behaviors might be and thus, where they may go.

The ten myths mentioned in this book come from the book *Premarital Sex in America* by Mark Regnerus and Jeremy Uecker. They call these ten things myths, in their own words: "because the empirical data from surveys and interviews suggests they aren't true most of the time. In other words, these ten myths may be believed by many emerging adult men and women, but the evidence supporting them just isn't there."

When Regnerus and Uecker speak about empirical data, what do they mean? How reliable is their data? Again in their own words:

> The majority of our survey findings come from the third wave of the National Longitudinal Study of Adolescent Health (Add Health), the largest, most extensive data set available about American young people. Add Health suits our purposes for a number of reasons. First, its interviewers asked a detailed set of questions not only about the respondents' sexual activity patterns, but about each romantic and/or sexual relationship reported by a respondent. Second, Add Health is a longitudinal "panel study" that allows us to track changes in respondents' own attitudes and behaviors over time. Respondents were questioned twice (waves 1 and 2) while they were in high school and then again (wave 3) when they were 18–28 years old. Each wave of Add Health includes a large number of respondents, and 15,197 completed the wave-3 survey (which took place between July 2001 and May 2002). When we

restricted our analyses only to those respondents who are no longer in high school and who are no older than 23, we were left with a working wave-3 sample size of 11,729.12 In addition to Add Health, we examined data from three other surveys: the National Survey of Family Growth (NSFG), the College Women's Survey (CWS), and the College Social Life Survey (CSLS). The NSFG is a nationally representative survey of Americans aged 15–44 that concentrates on fertility, health, and parenting. As such, the NSFG asked detailed questions about sexual behavior and includes a considerable number of emerging adults. Our working NSFG sample size of 2,580 young adults comes from the 2002 series of interviews. The CWS is a national study of college women conducted in the Winter of 2001 and directed by family scholars Norval Glenn (University of Texas at Austin) and Elizabeth Marquardt (Institute for American Values). Glenn and Marquardt's telephone survey of 1,000 college women focused on their attitudes, values, and behaviors with respect to sex, dating, and marriage. The online CSLS, directed by Stanford sociologist Paula England, has so far collected data from over 10,000 undergraduate students across numerous universities, spanning 2005–2008. While it is not representative of young adults—or even of college students—it is a valuable source of information and the most recent of the data sources. Because these three surveys are smaller than Add Health and cross-sectional in nature, we use them only when they address issues not adequately covered by Add Health.

The data Regnerus and Uecker analyzed was the most extensive available for the area of their interests. Note that these social scientists did not write a book about a theory of behavior among emerging adults. They did not set out with a hypothesis. They collected new data in the form of interviews with subjects, crunched the numbers from existing data sets, and reached conclusions that refute many of the working theories that young adults use to run their sex lives. In other words, lots of people observe the world they inhabit and form ideas about how sex works (theories) that are not in line with the experimental data.

Appendix C

More About The Ten Myths

As noted in the text of this book, *Premarital Sex in America*, by Mark Regnerus and Jeremy Uecker is the source of the 10 myths. It is a thoroughly researched book by highly qualified social scientists. It is also very accessible to the average reader and I recommend it to anyone wanting to dig further into the science of sexual relationships. Regnerus and Uecker did not organize their book around the 10 myths, and only mentioned them in their concluding chapter. While writing this book I compiled selected quotations from throughout PMSA. In this appendix I have placed them under the headings of each of the myths, along with some further data and thoughts on each of the 10.

Myth #1: Long term exclusivity is not possible or desirable.

Data: Long-term exclusivity (faithfulness to one partner) is possible and also what everyone says they want.

The first piece of data which disproves this myth is hidden in plain sight. As Regnerus and Uecker report in *Premarital Sex in America*, "When we ask our students in class how long half of all marriages last, they fumble around for a response, guessing five years, or seven or 10 tops…But the answer which never occurs to them, is a lifetime." Given the general vilification of marriage in most pop culture portrayals, we would think getting married only happens to fools or unfortunates who soon regret it. Even in this negative environment, 4 out of 5 adults over 25 years old are married (Pew Research Center Report of Social and Demographic Trends, 2012) (http://www.pewsocialtrends.org/2014/09/24/record-share-of-americans-have-never-married/#fn-19804-1).

How exclusive is our exclusivity? In other words, how faithful are we in marriage? Regnerus and Uecker, using the General Social Survey conducted every two years since 1972, put the rate of marital infidelity at 12-13%. In a 2013 article for Bloomberg.com, the numbers are quoted as 14.7% for women and 21% of men self reporting infidelity. While these numbers are not great, they still highlight the fact that most of us marry, stay married for life, and stay faithful within our marriages. This is what we want, and most of us achieve it.

Not only is long-term exclusivity possible, it is also what the vast majority of us want. In a 2013 Gallup survey, only 5% of Americans say they have never been married and never want to be married. Again, this statistic must be kept in the context of the overwhelmingly bad press marriage faces. The headline of the article from Gallup article reveals this bias: Most in U.S. Want Marriage, but It's Importance has Dropped. When only 5% of us have never been married and do not want to get married – meaning 95% of us either want to get married, are married, or were married previously – how much has marriage dropped in importance? (www.gallup.com/poll /163802/marriage-importance-dropped.aspx)

Myth #2: You have to introduce sex to sustain a new relationship or help a struggling relationship.

Data: Waiting to have sex is the best thing to do if you want a long term, stable relationship. The longer you wait to have sex the better your odds of sustaining your relationship.

This myth has the strongest influence upon us. Sex is portrayed in pop culture as such a singular good that it can create love and health in our relationships all by itself. The data suggests otherwise. It suggests that introducing sex early is not helpful if we want a long term relationship, and introducing sex into a struggling relationship is more likely to lead to negative outcomes.

Selected quotes from Regnerus and Ueker, *Premarital Sex in America*:

The reasons that Americans of all ages could give for their failed relationships are numerous, but one problem may uniquely plague emerging-adult relationships. It's the role of sex (rather than its presence): many couples lack a clear, shared, and suitable role for the sex they experience within a romantic relationship, especially when sex is introduced relatively early. Many interviewees testify that sex is often difficult to talk about, in part because the partners are still getting to know each other and deep conversation is considered too intimate. Yet **sex becomes a clear goal and new priority—the elephant in the corner that demands attention when they're together.**

It [sex] acquires an increasingly central role in the relationship while at the same time **other aspects of the relationship remain immature**.

One interviewee in another study lamented thus: "We were so distracted [by physical intimacy] towards the end, **just to cover our relationship**. We drifted apart, and some of the reason **we were dragging it out was because of the physical touch**. I think that I would have been thinking a lot more clearly without that."

Apart from relationship security, familiarity, and a shared domicile, **sex has a difficult time playing a supportive role in fostering intimacy and building love**. Instead, it wants to be the lead character. But when left to sustain a relationship, sex typically falters.

First, sex within their sporadic interactions began to

claim a place and priority that outstripped its natural boundaries. In most marriages and cohabitations, even in the honeymoon phase, sex plays a supporting role to the mundane activities of normal life. **In a relationship where two people are not sharing lots of normal life activities—a scenario common among young adults—sex can quickly take center stage.**

Clearly sex does not stabilize or create relationships, the two things we most expect it to do. And this wreaks havoc. Another researcher, Dean Busby, of Brigham Young University's School of Family Life conducted a study among a pool of 20,000 couples. His team reported:

> "Couples who had sex the earliest — such as after the first date or within the first month of dating — had the worst relationship outcomes. What seems to happen is that **if couples become sexual too early, this very rewarding area of the relationship overwhelms good decision-making** and keeps couples in a relationship that might not be the best for them in the long-run,"

Busby and his colleagues published their 2010 study in the Journal of Family Psychology. The study was supported by research grants from the School of Family Life and the Family Studies Center at Brigham Young University (www.sciencedaily.com/releases)

A last quote from *Premarital Sex in America* sums this up perfectly:

> Perhaps emerging adults are lonelier than we think and are convinced that sex, with its connectional characteristics, is the glue that will cinch together something good and create a relationship that ought to endure—even if it doesn't

Myth #3: The sexual double standard (men and women experience sex uniquely) is inherently wrong and must be resisted by any means.

Data: The sexual double standard is inherently human because men and women are unique in their sexuality and experience sex accordingly. Trying to make women treat sex the way men treat sex or make men treat sex the way women treat sex is not going to work. It's like trying to get a dolphin and a horse to experience water in the same way.

Men and women are different in fundamental ways. When women are told to approach sex in the same way a man would approach sex (presumably as a low cost, low risk, physical experience of pleasure) the outcomes are negative. As Regnerus and Uecker say in *Premarital Sex in America* "Woman may enjoy sex as much as men do, but on average they don't pursue it as often or for the same reasons."

In their 2002 article "The Casualties of Casual Sex," Psychologists Elizabeth Paul and Kristen Hayes note women's mixed emotions in their study of casual sex and regret: "Although some women may have experienced positive emotions during the sexual encounter (i.e., feeling chosen, noticed, attractive), they are more likely (than men) to feel ashamed and regretful afterwards."

Selected quotes from Regnerus and Uecker's *Premarital Sex in America*:

> "When we examine simple connections between recent and lifetime sexual partnering, frequency of sex, and a variety of emotional-health indicators— including depression scales, self-reported episodic crying, life satisfaction, depression diagnoses, and current use of prescription antidepressants—it quickly becomes apparent that having more numerous sexual partners is associated with poorer emotional states in women, but not men.

> There's a linear association between both lifetime

117

and recent partners and indicators of poorer emotional health, and women who report the greatest number of partners display the clearest symptoms of depression."

Men's sexual partnership and behavior patterns, on the other hand, display no clear associations with any depressive symptoms...Among those who report the highest number (more than 10) of lifetime or recent sexual partners, just 11% say they've ever been diagnosed with depression – three to four times lower than among women.

Myth #4: Men can't be expected to abide by the sexual rules women may wish to set.

Data: Men will abide by the sexual rules women set. Women are the sexual gatekeepers and can determine their own terms for when sex should start in a relationship. Men will wait or not wait depending upon what the majority of women decide to do.

A study published in The Journal of Sex Research by Laurie Choen and Lance Shotland revealed that when women thought sex should start having sex in a relationship and when they actually did have sex showed an 88% correlation. For men, the number was 19% correlation, meaning that their wishes about when sex beings are statistically insignificant. (www.tandfonline.com)

In consensual sexual relationships, the "consent" is given overwhelmingly by the woman. The fact is that women have the power to set the terms they want for sex, but they don't do this in a vacuum. Perception of power on the part of a woman is affected by the sexual marketplace she and everyone around her inhabit.

So while women decide when sex starts in their relationships they feel a tremendous amount of pressure to introduce sex into those relationships based upon what they perceive as "normal" sexual behavior around them.

Myth #5: It doesn't matter what other people do sexually; you make your own decisions.

Data: It matters very much what other people do sexually. When many women flood the sexual marketplace with relatively low cost, low commitment sex, and when many men access cheap pornographic sex, everyone is affected. Based upon what people are doing sexually today, new norms are established and the market adjusts to the new conditions.

Sexual Economics Theory posited by Sociologists Roy Baumeister and Kathleen Vohs, basically states that sex is an asset controlled by women, which men purchase in the marketplace of relationships. A full explanation of the theory here: http://search.bwh.harvard.edu/concourse

This is a theory that shows a great deal of promise even though it draws a lot of criticism for over-simplification and misrepresenting women's interest in sex for pleasure's sake. A prime example of this criticism here: http://www.huffingtonpost.com/2011/09/19/sex-and-love-simple-econo_n_970408.html

Theories are only valuable if they hold up to scrutiny when data is collected, and they tend to fall apart rather quickly if the data obviously disproves them. Sexual Economics Theory may not sound right to some people, and may appear to reduce every sexual relationship to pimp and prostitute to others, but it is not disproven by the data. In fact, the data gives enough credence to the theory that we should not ignore it when it comes to explaining sexual behavior. According to Regnerus and Ueker: Baumeister and Vohs's [Sexual Economics] Theory is "impressive and convincing [and] some of its key aspects reinforced by literally dozens of studies."

Myth #6: Porn doesn't affect your relationships.

Data: Porn will definitely affect your relationships, and actually affects all our relationships through affecting perception and expectations for sexual activity.

Indiana University professor Dolf Zillmann, an authority on the effects of pornography says in his paper "Influence of Unrestrained Access to Erotica on Adolescents' and Young Adults' Dispositions toward Sexuality," published in the Journal of Adolescent Health, prolonged exposure to pornography leads people to:

- overestimate the popularity and pleasure of less common forms of sexual behavior

- presume that sexual exclusivity is both unrealistic and uncommon in real life

- believe that sexual inactivity is actually bad for one's health

- hold cynical attitudes about love, affection, and marriage/family

Selected quotes from Regnerus and Ueker's *Premarital Sex in America*:

> [Porn] encourages women as well as men to have sex earlier than they otherwise might have. Sounds crazy, right? It's not. One of the obvious concerns about porn is that it functions for men as a substitute for a real person, and women realize this. It can curb men's ability to relate to women by diminishing their interest—and perhaps more importantly their patience—in doing so.

> Since high-speed digital porn gives men additional attractive sexual options—more supply for his demand—it by definition takes some measure of price control away from women. As a result, the cost of real sex can only go down, taking men's interest in making steep relationship commitments with it.

Myth #7: Everyone else is having more sex than you are.

Data: Everyone else is not having more sex than you are having, even though everyone believes everyone else is having more sex than they are having.

Selected quotes from Regnerus and Uecker's *Premarital Sex in America*:

In study after study—as well as in our interviews— emerging adults think that other people are having more sex than they are.

Overestimates of others' sexual behavior are found in Bogle, Hooking Up; Tracy A. Lambert, Arnold S. Kahn, and Kevin J. Apple, "Pluralistic Ignorance and Hooking Up," The Journal of Sex Research 40 (2003): 129–33; Page, Hammermeister, and Scanlan, "Everybody's Not Doing It"; Paul and Hayes, "The Casualties of 'Casual' Sex"; and Pamela C. Regan and Carla S. Dreyer, "Lust? Love? Status? Young Adults' Motives for Engaging in Casual Sex," Journal of Psychology & Human Sexuality 11 (1999): 1–24.

The results of pluralistic ignorance about others' sex lives, however, can "lead one or both sexual partners to act according to the perceived norm rather than to their own convictions." In other words, sex becomes a self-fulfilling prophecy: **"The more students believe sexual activity is occurring, the more sexual activity occurs."** (Tracy A. Lambert, Arnold S. Kahn, and Kevin J. Apple, "Pluralistic Ignorance and Hooking Up," The Journal of Sex Research 40 (2003): 129–33)

In a study of over 700 undergraduates, researchers noted that men who considerably overestimated the sexual activity of their male peers were also 11 times more likely to have had sexual intercourse in the past month than were those who underestimated men's sexual activity. (Page, Hammermeister, and Scanlan, "Everybody's Not Doing It")

This is another instance where the data lines up with sexual economics theory. When people perceive the amount and price of sex "on the market" in certain ways, they will "shop" and "sell" according to those perceptions.

Myth #8: Sex doesn't have to mean anything.

Data: Sex means something, always, every time, without exception, even if a single sexual act appears to have no meaning, because the accumulation of sexual acts affects us.

This is the second most powerful myth, only beat out by Myth #2. It has roots in several other myths and it is extremely difficult for many of us to grasp. Even when we personally experience the effect of sexual relationships and believe sex is meaningful for us, we are so inundated with stories of casual sex which is nothing more than "good, clean fun" that we think we must be the exception. We must take sex too seriously. This is not true, especially if you are female.

Selected quotes from Regnerus and Ueker, *Premarital Sex in America*:

> Psychologists Elizabeth Paul and Kristen Hayes note women's mixed emotions in their study of casual sex and regret: "Although some women may have experienced positive emotions during the sexual encounter (i.e., feeling chosen, noticed, attractive), they are more likely to feel ashamed and regretful afterwards." (Page 658 in Elizabeth L. Paul and Kristen A. Hayes, "The Casualties of 'Casual' Sex: A Qualitative Exploration of the Phenomenology of College Students' Hookups," Journal of Social and Personal Relationships 19, no. 5 (2002): 639–61.)

> When we examine simple connections between recent and lifetime sexual partnering, frequency of sex, and a variety of emotional-health indicators—

including depression scales, self-reported episodic crying, life satisfaction, depression diagnoses, and current use of prescription antidepressants—it quickly becomes apparent that having more numerous sexual partners is associated with poorer emotional states in women, but not men.

There's a linear association between both lifetime and recent partners and indicators of poorer emotional health, and women who report the greatest number of partners display the clearest symptoms of depression.

Depression diagnoses run just under 50 percent among those who'd had more than 10 partners in the past year.

Among those with a more extensive sexual history, there's nothing about having had seven sexual partners that necessarily makes one feel worse than having had six, or 12 versus 10. Rather, as our analyses indicate, it is in the general adding of partners that the problem lies; amassing sexual partners betrays a lack of relationship security. There is no magic number of partners to avoid other than "more."

Even getting married—deciding to settle down with only one sex partner for good—doesn't erase the emotional challenges for women who've had numerous sex partners in their lifetime. While no association with depressive symptoms is apparent among now-married young women who've had up to four sex partners in their lifetime, problems appear among those who've had 5–10, and even more among those who've had more than 10 partners (results not shown). On all six outcomes, such women display more intense emotional difficulties. Among those who've had more than 10 partners, 41 percent report being depressed at least some time in the past seven days. Just over 14 percent are actively taking antidepressants, and only 79 percent say they're satisfied or very satisfied with their life. So while the security of a marital relationship can diminish sex-related emotional-health problems, it doesn't often take them away.

While the data does not indicate the same level of negative emotional outcomes among men, we might fail to recognize the most obvious effect sexual activity has upon men: the women, who are affected by sexual activity, will be married to men who will have to deal with both their partner's sexual history *and* the way their own sexual history impacts their partner.

Myth #9: Marriage can always wait and should wait until we are stable and/or successful.

Data: Marriage can't wait forever. There is a market of marriageable people and it decreases over time leaving less and less desirable candidates available, while we ourselves become less attractive candidates.

All the survey data collected over the longest period of time shows that married people are more economically, emotionally, and sexually stable. They make more money. They are happier. They have more sex. The data also shows that trying out sexual partners doesn't make us more stable as singles or as marrieds. The game most emerging adults are playing is a cat chasing its tail. the success and stability they want comes from being the kind of people who commit and work but they inhabit a world where commitment and hard work (at least when it comes to relationships) is something that will happen "some day." Meanwhile they practice non-committal until it becomes habitual and normal. When it comes time to "settle down" they have no idea how to do it.

Selected quotes from Regnerus and Ueker's *Premarital Sex in America*:

The losers in this discounted sexual marketplace are clearly women who would prefer a high price for sex: those who want to remain virgins until marriage (and yet who wish to get married). **They are increasingly put in a bind in their pursuit of a lifelong relationship, constrained by how the sexual decisions of their peers alter market expectations about the price of sex.** Many feel pressure to "take what they can get" and commence a sexual relationship with a marriage-minded man before marriage, or risk the real possibility that in holding out for a chaste man to marry they will wait a lot longer than they would like to, watching the pool of available, ideal men shrink before their eyes.

An increasing number of young men and women are having a difficult time discerning exactly how to generate a secure relationship and what it might look like. When we talk about marriage in the classroom and describe its relative security, most—especially women—like what they hear. They want it for themselves. But **how they get from where they're at to where they'd like to go is often a big mystery.** And most young men have no interest in helping them find it at present.

Most sexual relationships among emerging adults neither begin with marital intentions nor end in marriage or even cohabitation. They just begin and end. **Reasons for their termination are numerous, of course, but one overlooked possibility is that many of them don't know how to get or stay married to the kind of person they'd like to find.** For not a few, their parents provided them with a glimpse into married life, and what they saw at the dinner table—if they dined with their parents much at all—didn't look very inviting. They hold the institution of marriage in high regard, and they put considerable pressure— probably too much—on what their own eventual marriage ought to look like. And yet it seems that there is little effort from any institutional source aimed at helping emerging adults consider how their present social, romantic, and sexual experiences shape or war against their vision of marriage—or even how marriage might fit in with their other life goals. In fact, talk of career goals seems increasingly divorced from the relational context in which many emerging adults may eventually find themselves. **They speak of the MDs, JDs, and PhDs they intend to acquire with far more confidence than they speak of committed relationships or marriage**

In a meta-analysis of *five different surveys* that explored marriage outcomes, researchers note that respondents who marry between ages 22 and 25 express greater marital satisfaction than do those who marry later than that. **In other words the conventional wisdom about the obvious benefits (to marital happiness) of delayed marriage overreaches.**

All these findings, however, are largely lost on emerging adults because of the compelling power of the popular notion in America that marriages carry a 50 percent risk of divorce. End of story. Indeed, what matters most is what people think reality is like, not how reality really is. **Human beings think and act based on what they believe to be true, often with little regard to alternative possibilities that may stick closer to empirical accuracies.** They have faith in the conventional wisdom about marriage—and especially about early marriage. Consequently, marriage is considered off-limits to many emerging adults, especially those in the middle of college or building a career. Thus while research suggests that adults who are married and in monogamous relationships report more global happiness, more physical satisfaction with sex, and more emotional satisfaction with sex, emerging adults don't believe it. Such claims just don't feel true. And why should they? When's the last time you watched a romantic film about a happily married 40-year-old couple?

Sociologist Monica Gaughan's study of 341 women in their late 20s revealed that the search-theory explanation of marital timing may not always work out so well in reality. In fact, women who had more numerous sexual relationships during their early adult years, who spent more time in such relationships, and who had additional sexual liaisons besides their romantic relationships were all less likely to be married at the time of the interview. Gaughan concludes that "more is not better," if the goal of relationships is to search for an optimal marital match. That isn't every woman's goal, of course. But if it is, the chemistry-search strategy doesn't work as well as many believe it does.

While we can't assess exactly why the more sexually experienced emerging adults are divorcing at a rate well above their less-experienced peers, two processes are potential suspects. First, it might be that memories of past sexual experiences intrude upon the sexual lives of the married partners. These memories could be good ones (which make their marital sex seem inferior in comparison) or bad ones (which could still color the marital sex in negative ways). Second, the repeated practice of sex without long-term commitment might make committed sex seem foreign or boring and make an exciting sex life difficult to integrate into a bonded, committed relationship. Settling down can be hard to do.

Myth #10: Moving in together is definitely a step toward marriage.

Data: Moving in together is not necessarily a step toward marriage and is more likely to lead to break up than to marriage.

Why would cohabitation lead to better marital outcomes? Most cohabitation scenarios do not involve couples who are ready to commit to each other. Living together leaves one or both partners in a state of "auditioning" for the part of permanent partner. Have you ever been to an audition? What are you doing when you audition for a part? You are putting your best foot forward. You are presenting yourself in the best possible light. You are trying to appear worthy of getting the part. None of these things bear much of a resemblance to loving relationships.

Selected quotes from Regnerus and Ueker's *Premarital Sex in America*:

> A common scenario in many emerging-adult sexual relationships evolves like this: "I think probably one of the reasons I broke up is that ... **we were having issues, and I didn't feel that we were a married couple, so I didn't feel the need to work them out.**

> Between 50 and 70 percent of couples today are thought to be cohabitating before marrying. Around 15 percent of all 18-23 year olds in the Add Health study said they were currently cohabitating, and nearly 60 percent of the study's women had cohabited at least once before age. As a path to marriage, however, such arrangements are unreliable: **about one in five actually results in a marriage.**

> In a study of the reasons people give for cohabiting, couples who cited intimacy-based reasons—like wishing to spend more time with each other—were among those most likely to stay together, followed by those who elected to cohabit for practical reasons like combining expenses. **Couples who were out to "test" their relationship, however, failed far**

more often.

Although research conclusions may seem hostile to cohabitation, there's nothing inherently political about the results. **These are simply the empirical patterns from numerous studies conducted by many different researchers using a variety of datasets. And they generally point to more pessimistic conclusions about cohabitation.** Sure, not every cohabiting experience will turn sour or nix someone's hopes of marrying a partner. In the world of sociological generalizations, there are always plenty of examples that don't fit the trend. But exceptions only prove what's possible, not what's probable

Study Guide

How to Use This Study Guide

Often we are hindered from real discussions about sex because of our past experiences or because we find it an embarrassing subject. It is awkward for most of us to talk about sex, but that doesn't mean we shouldn't. The Bible has a consistent message about sex; it isn't dirty or something to avoid – it is a created thing that is good and meant for enjoyment when it is kept within God's prescription for its use. Because of it's ability to deceive us, we need to talk about sex with others who will help us see into our blind spots - we need help to get the elephant into our bar. Don't go it alone as an individual or as a couple, get another couple or another person to go with you.

This study must be conducted with sensitivity and respect. No one should feel compelled to speak about their sexuality or sexual experiences. Members of the study must decide for themselves what to share and when to share it. We've all been in groups formal or informal where someone tries to "one up" the last story told. Don't be that person. Think about others in the group and weigh whether or not your contribution could help them rather than adding something you think will help you or make you look good. Be willing to laugh at your own expense before laughing at the expense of someone else. Sex provides many incongruities, which make us, laugh and there is no need to talk about it as if we are solving the greatest problems facing humanity. On the other hand, humor about sex is often a mask lust wears as an excuse to probe others for its own satisfaction. Don't be the person who tries to push the discussion further with a joke in order to excite lust in yourself or others. Sex is funny. Lust is not funny.

Leading The Study

The ideal leaders for a group study are a married man and woman who are comfortable in their own skin, who are willing to be transparent about their struggles with sex, past and present, and who are willing to learn along with everyone else. If a couple is not available to lead a coed group, the study should be led by a man for a group of men or a woman for a group of women. A group should not be more than 7 or 8 couples or 10 – 12 individuals. In smaller groups 2 -3 men or women with a leader of the same gender, or an older couple with a younger couple can use this study.

The primary responsibility of anyone leading the group is to establish a safe environment. Use the first meeting of the study to spell out expectations of confidentiality. Ask members to agree to keep details about discussions to themselves. Tell the group you will not allow the discussion to get out of hand. Explain the idea of laughter versus lusty humor. Assure members they do not have to reveal any personal details; that they will not be "put on the spot" during group sessions. Create and communicate avenues for participants to contact you privately about issues they feel uncomfortable sharing with the whole group. Let members voice questions and concerns about the subject matter. In coed groups establish rules for communication that allow male and female members to communicate with their same gender leaders.

Leaders should prepare themselves for this study by reading the book and considering the discussion questions. Leaders need to decide the level of transparency they can tolerate in their own lives and, if they are part of a couple they need to discuss this with their partner ahead of time so both agree on what to share and what not to share.

Your goal in leading this group is to establish a safe space where people have the opportunity to explore their experience with sex and relationships and encounter the truth. Safe space includes:

- a reasonable expectation of confidentiality

- time for every person to speak.

- respect for what each person contributes.

- protecting people from themselves when they over-communicate.

- protecting the integrity of the group by keeping the discussion civil and meaningful at all times.

- keeping the group on schedule.

When group members start taking ownership of the group they will begin to do these things without your intervention. Be patient and consistent and your group has the chance to start working. Realize from the outset every group member comes to the group with different experiences and expectations. Some will have great revelations, others may not seem to get much from it. Just be faithful and real. Let the Truth work on you no matter what happens in the group.

Each week contains an opening statement, a prayer, discussion questions, a Bible reference, and questions for reflection. The overall theme of the book and study is the deception of sex and the truth of the gospel. Use the questions to further the group's discovery of both. There is no need to cover each question in each group time, or to memorize each Bible verse. Pray for God to lead the group, reveal deception and truth. Listen for moments of revelation and be ready to linger in them. Give God room to work and expect him to do it. Ask group members to honestly reflect on the revelations they receive and to share them with the group.

Learn More About the Elephant

One of the great advantages of our time is the ability to connect with people and stories over vast differences in distance, background, age, and experiences. We can pick up a book and read it in a reading and learning community. If you are reading this in its Kindle format you can see passages other people find interesting or noteworthy enough to highlight and you can choose to share your highlights with other readers. If you want to take this a step further as you interact with this book and study guide, visit our online community for The Elephant in the Bar at www.TheElephantInTheBar.com. There you will discover more resources for leading group studies, current stories about sex in pop culture, and a forum to share your insights and read what others are learning

Week 1 - Introduction

Sex. All by itself it is a powerful word. There is no doubt sex bends things. We may or may not think we are sexually driven as individuals, but we are in a culture filled with people who are highly influenced by sex. This fact alone makes an honest discussion about sex both difficult and necessary.

Prayer

God, if you are anything you are true. As we meet together please show us if we are deceived and show us your truth. Help us to be open and honest before you and with each other.

Scripture

The wisdom of the prudent is to discern his way, but the folly of fools is deceiving. (Proverbs 14:8)

Discussion Questions

1. What one word would you use to describe sex?

2. What do you think our culture's opinion about sex is?

3. What factors contributed to your thoughts and feelings about sex? (parents, siblings, television, movies, peers) Where these positive or negative influences?

4. Do you have any sexual experiences that cause feelings of confusion, doubt, fear or shame? What, if anything, have you done to resolve these feelings?

5. Is it possible you have been deceived about the value and purpose of sex? What makes you think you have (or have not) been deceived about sex?

Reflection

1. What one thing did you hear during this group time that surprised you?

2. Did you feel the discussion was useful? Could it have been better? How?

3. At any time during the discussion did you feel like you should share something but held back? If yes, why did you hold back?

4. Do you sense God's presence in this group? If yes, in what way?

5. What should you share with the group in the next meeting?

Week 2 - Chapter One
Ten Myths We Believe about Sex and Relationships

Opening

Are you skeptical? Do you need proof? Getting information and answers can be good, but it doesn't always help us. Many times the more answers we get, the more questions it generates. And when we get data that contradicts our beliefs we rarely drop our beliefs like hot potatoes. We question the data. Do you see how data, and information, and belief are not so clearly defined as we'd like them to be? Our beliefs about sex and relationships are hard to separate from the data. It takes courage to be open to new possibilities.

Prayer

God, we confess our desire for answers. You have all answers, but you decide what we need to know and when we need to know it. Please help us to see the answers you have given.

Scripture

I call upon you, for you will answer me, O God; incline your ear to me; hear my words. (Psalm 17:6)

Discussion Questions

1. What roles do you play? What roles do you see others playing? (Some roles to consider: the good girl, the jock, the smart one, the funny one, the hero, the goat, the winner, the loser, the artist, the tough guy, the girlie girl, the achiever) Where did these roles come from?

2. Have you ever done something because it "fit the script" rather than because you actually wanted to do it? (some examples: went to college even though you hate school work, took a risk because your peers expect you to be outrageous, drank too much because you are the party animal, studied way too long because you are the smart one)

3. Of the ten myths about sex and relationships, which one is most believable to you? Which myth would you least want to debunk?

4. If a fully consenting couple filmed their sexual activities for their own private use, would you consider it to be pornography? Why or why not? What constitutes pornography? Is pornography affecting your relationships? How?

5. Do we act rationally when it comes to sex and relationships or do we act irrationally? Are we encouraged to act rationally or irrationally by examples in our media (i.e. music, movies, books)?

Reflection

1. What one thing did you hear during this group time that surprised you?

2. Did you feel the discussion was useful? Could it have been better? How?

3. At any time during the discussion did you feel like you should share something but held back? If yes, why did you hold back?

4. Do you sense God's presence in this group? If yes, in what way?

5. What should you share with the group in the next meeting?

Week 3 - Chapter Two
Sex in the Wild Kingdom

Opening

The essence of sex is all around us; in grocery store check out lines peering out from magazine covers, and in any segment of television we watch. But the fact of sex is still stark and private. People don't watch pornography on minivan DVD players. Couples don't copulate on street corners. Even prostitutes use hotel rooms. Why are we the only species that both glorifies and conceals sex?

Prayer

God, you are the author of all life, and you made us in your image. Please show us how being made in your image affects the way we relate to each other physically, mentally, and spiritually.

Scripture

So God created man in his own image, in the image of God he created him; male and female he created them. (Genesis 1:27)

Discussion Questions

1. What would you do if you encountered a couple have sex in a public place? Would your react differently if they were young teenagers or college age?

2. How would you account for the way human beings treat sexuality differently from any other species?

3. Do you think there are right and wrong ways of having sex? Why?

4. What is the purpose of sex?

Reflection

1. What one thing did you hear during this group time that surprised you?

2. Did you feel the discussion was useful? Could it have been better? How?

3. At any time during the discussion did you feel like you should share something but held back? If yes, why did you hold back?

4. Do you sense God's presence in this group? If yes, in what way?

5. What should you share with the group in the next meeting?

Week 4 - Chapter Three
Sex in the Kingdom

Opening

We've been meeting several weeks now and talking about sex. Is it getting any easier? Less awkward? Probably not. Comedians can stand on stage and say the most outrageous things related to sex and we can watch movies and television shows portraying sex, but it is entirely different to have a face-to-face discussion about sex with real people who aren't making it into a joke.

Prayer

God, you created sex and you created us. You know how hard it is for us to have a real discussion about sex. Please lead us now into your truth and show us how to talk about your creation in a way that helps us grow into the people you want us to be.

Scripture

Open my eyes, that I may behold wondrous things out of your law. (Psalm 119:18)

Discussion Questions

1. Did you ever have "the talk" about sex with someone (a parent, an older sibling, etc.)? What was it like? Do you think it's ok to talk about sex in a mixed gender group? Why or why not?

2. When reading the Bible's explicit language and imagery about sex, how does it make you feel?

3. How does your church/religious background compare to the actual words of the Bible?

4. What are the implications of the Bible's teaching about sex as something pleasurable to be enjoyed and not simply biological to procreate?

Reflection

1. What one thing did you hear during this group time that surprised you?

2. Did you feel the discussion was useful? Could it have been better? How?

3. At any time during the discussion did you feel like you should share something but held back? If yes, why did you hold back?

4. Do you sense God's presence in this group? If yes, in what way?

5. What should you share with the group in the next meeting?

Week 5 - Chapter Four
Sex in a Box?

Opening

No sex outside of marriage. Try that on for size. Say it out loud. It seems as if this particular idea is not only unpopular, it is ridiculous, and perhaps it is even hateful. The abstinence movement is the subject of jokes and ridicule. Despite the opinions flooding us, no proof of any sort has ever been offered to prove that staying away from sex does us any harm. On the contrary, the evidence points to marriage as the best place to have sex.

Prayer

God, we don't know why you created marriage and why placed sex only in the context of marriage. Show us what we need to know about both and teach us about yourself through your all your created things.

Scripture

Turn my eyes from looking at worthless things; and give me life in your ways. (Psalm 119:37)

Discussion Questions

1. How long do half of all marriages last? (warning, trick question, you need to really think about this)

2. What is the attitude of your friends about marriage? Does marriage ruin a relationship? Does it ruin sex?

3. Did anyone ever tell you it was better to wait until you got married to have sex? Would you tell a friend to wait? Why or why not?

4. If you are having sex outside of marriage, would you consider stopping? What would happen if you stopped having sex outside marriage?

5. If the Bible's teaching about marriage is true, what are the implications for us? What does this do to our ideas about sex? Does Christian doctrine make the way for sex to be more enjoyable or less enjoyable?

Reflection

1. What one thing did you hear during this group time that surprised you?

2. Did you feel the discussion was useful? Could it have been better? How?

3. At any time during the discussion did you feel like you should share something but held back? If yes, why did you hold back?

4. Do you sense God's presence in this group? If yes, in what way?

5. What should you share with the group in the next meeting?

Week 6 - Chapter Five
Sex Sells. Should We Buy?

Opening

We human beings have a habit of believing our time on earth is the most significant time in history. Whatever is happening is the biggest or best or worst. Sexuality seems like it has never been so hard to navigate as it is in today's environment. The truth is much more complex. Sex has a history of use and abuse with humanity, and people in all ages and cultures have had to face the challenges associated with sex and relationships. Acting as if our problems are unique and/or insurmountable using ancient wisdom (i.e. the Bible) cuts us off from tried and true solutions.

Prayer

God, you've seen the whole history of humanity and you know how sex has fooled us. Open our hearts to follow true things until they lead all the way to you, The Truth.

Scripture

Sanctify them in the truth; your word is truth.

(John 17:17)

Discussion Questions

1. Name the three most ridiculous items you've seen associated with sexual imagery.

2. Have you ever been the victim of a planned out deception? (practical jokes, someone trying to steal your identity, anyone who has ever participated in a time-share presentation...) Was there an element of truth that got you hooked? How did it make you feel when you discovered the deception? How did you find out?

3. Have you ever felt like an "untouchable"? What did you do to try to get rid of the feeling? Did it work?

4. Does something or someone in your life make you feel special? What do they do? Would you still feel special if they stopped doing it?

5. Do you know people who are not right for each other, but they stay together because of sex? How does it make you feel to see a friend in a relationship like this? Why can you see it better than they do?

Reflection

1. What one thing did you hear during this group time that surprised you?

2. Did you feel the discussion was useful? Could it have been better? How?

3. At any time during the discussion did you feel like you should share something but held back? If yes, why did you hold back?

4. Do you sense God's presence in this group? If yes, in what way?

5. What should you share with the group in the next meeting?

Week 7 - Chapter Six
The Gospel Elephant

Opening

The next time you go to a wedding, instead of watching the bride walking down the aisle, watch the groom when he sees the bride coming to him. We don't use the word "adoration" much any more, but that is the best way to describe how a groom looks at a bride. It is absolute approval, acceptance, and desire packed into a glance. Being on the receiving end of adoration is unlike anything. It is life flowing into us. The more highly we think of the one doing the adoring the more life it gives. The Christian gospel is that all human beings can receive this look from the Most High.

Prayer

God, look upon us with your life-giving gaze. Show us all the places we've looked to find ourselves adored and show us how much you want us to find ourselves adored in your eyes.

Scripture

For your Maker is your husband, the Lord of hosts is his name; and the Holy One of Israel is your Redeemer, the God of the whole earth he is called. (Isaiah 54:5)

Discussion Questions

1. How does the biblical metaphor of God being the husband to his people make you feel? Do you react differently if you are a man or a woman?

2. Many people have the impression that Christianity leads to low self esteem because it talks about people being sinners, or lost, or displeasing to God. How does this appear in the light of the gospel message that God wants to come into full contact with us and stay with us? What would happen to you if you really believed God called you clean? How would it change your self image?

3. The word sanctified can mean "set apart." How does the thought of being set apart by God and for God make you feel? Is it a good thing to be set apart? Does it separate us from other people?

4. We all believe rape is wrong. Why is it wrong? Try to defend this position without appealing to absolute Morality (i.e. God). If we admit to the existence of absolute right and wrong – for example that rape is always wrong no matter the circumstances – we must admit the possibility that there may be standards about all behavior that we may or may not agree with. What do you use to justify your ideas about sex?

5. For a moment imagine the gospel is real. God wants you to feel completely clean, completely special, and completely right, and he found the way to do it through the life, death, burial and resurrection of Jesus Christ. Would you embrace his plan? Why or why not? What would be the catch?

Reflection

1. What one thing did you hear during this group time that surprised you?

2. Did you feel the discussion was useful? Could it have been better? How?

3. At any time during the discussion did you feel like you should share something but held back? If yes, why did you hold back?

4. Do you sense God's presence in this group? If yes, in what way?

5. What should you share with the group in the next meeting?

Week 8 - Chapter Seven
Married with Elephants

Opening

Marriage is both worshiped and scorned today. Those who commonly mock marriage and talk of it as a curse or outdated get married like the rest of us. Weddings are costly and so are divorces, everyone knows this, but marriage costs more than either. The vows we make should clue us in to the cost. The promises are the most extravagant we will ever utter. If we take them seriously, and we should, we should realize we need help.

Prayer

God, according to the Bible, marriage was your idea. Show us what you want it to be and help us to know what it can do and what it cannot.

Scripture

Let marriage be held in honor among all (Hebrews 13:4)

Questions for Discussion

1. Do you see yourself getting married someday? If you are married, did you always assume you were going to get married? Why? What was/is the appeal of getting married?

2. In your opinion is married sex better and more frequent that sex outside of marriage? What are the advantages of being married when it comes to sex? What are the disadvantages?

3. Did you feel safe the first time you had sex? Did you feel like you were trying to get away with something? Did you talk someone into having sex with you by trying to make them feel safe? Did someone make you feel safe enough to have sex with them? Consider how security impacts our sex lives.

4. Are you good at sex? How do you know you are good at sex? If you have doubts about your sexual performance how can you get reliable feedback? How can you get better at sex? What would be the best environment for getting better at sex? A committed monogamous marriage? Or series of semi-committed lovers?

5. What does it mean to "fear Christ"? What are some ways we can learn to fear Christ? How will we know when we are living in the fear of Christ?

Reflection

1. What one thing did you hear during this group time that surprised you?

2. Did you feel the discussion was useful? Could it have been better? How?

3. At any time during the discussion did you feel like you should share something but held back? If yes, why did you hold back?

4. Do you sense God's presence in this group? If yes, in what way?

5. What should you share with the group in the next meeting?

Week 9 - Chapter Eight
No God, No Glory

Opening

What would the world be like if everyone was full? Really full? If people knew they were completely loved and accepted it would change everything. The world economy would drastically change. Advertising would almost cease to exist as we know it. Governments and governing would change radically as contentment reigned in both leaders and the people they lead. The gospel claims this kind of fullness exists, not in sex or relationships with others, but first in a relationship with God.

Prayer

God you said you came to earth so that we could be full of life. Show us how we can have your glory in our lives all the time.

Scripture

And the Word became flesh and dwelt among us, and we have seen his glory; glory as of the only Son from the Father, full of grace and truth. (John 1:14)

Questions for Discussion

1. Would you describe your life as "full"? In your opinion what are the key elements of a full life? Can you name someone who appears to have a full life? What makes you say they have a full life?

2. Did you get married in a church/do you intend to get married in a church with a minister? Why?

3. What is glory? What is the most glorious thing in your life? Can it be taken away from you? How can you keep it?

4. Do you believe a person can have a great life; a fulfilling life, without ever experiencing sex?

Reflection

1. What one thing did you hear during this group time that surprised you?

2. Did you feel the discussion was useful? Could it have been better? How?

3. At any time during the discussion did you feel like you should share something but held back? If yes, why did you hold back?

4. Do you sense God's presence in this group? If yes, in what way?

5. How can you use what you've learned in this group to make the world (your home, your school, your work place, your community) a better place?

Week 10 – Chapter Nine
The Cure for Sexual Vertigo

Opening

The Sexual Revolution has become the sexual spin cycle. It makes us dizzy and confused and wondering how to get off the spinning ride. Once we see what sex has done to us we need to take definite steps to get our lives back. Confession is the tool we use to find ourselves and others and to become stable in a culture full of sexual gravity.

Prayer

God, give each of us the courage to share our hearts with you and each other, to ask for help where we need it, and to invite you into our whole lives.

Scripture

Therefore confess your sins to each other and pray for each other so that you may be healed. The prayer of a righteous person is powerful and effective. James 5:16

Questions for Discussion

1. Have you ever confessed something that you were afraid to confess? What happened?

2. Is there something you would be afraid to confess right now to anyone? Imagine living without that fear. How does it feel?

3. Has someone ever confessed something serious to you? How did you react? How did it make you feel?

4. If the gospel is true and you believed it completely, how would it affect your ability to both confess and hear confession?

Reflection

1. What one thing did you hear during this group time that surprised you?

2. Did you feel the discussion was useful? Could it have been better? How?

3. At any time during the discussion did you feel like you should share something but held back? If yes, why did you hold back?

4. Do you sense God's presence in this group? If yes, in what way?

5. What should you share with the group in the next meeting?